Twayne's United States Authors Series

Sylvia E. Bowman, *Editor*

INDIANA UNIVERSITY

Donald Davidson

Donald Davidson

By Thomas Daniel Young

Vanderbilt University

and

M. Thomas Inge

Virginia Commonwealth University

 190

Twayne Publishers, Inc. : : New York

For Arlease and Betty

PREFACE

In a literary career spanning more than forty years, Donald Davidson was poet, literary and social critic, historian, editor, teacher, and man of letters. Since the authors' intent is to provide a judicious introduction to his life and work, detailed analyses of all his literary creations have not been possible. Within the necessary space limitations, however, explication and discussion of representative selections from each literary genre have been offered. A disproportianate amount of space is used in the analysis of his poetry because less has been written about it than about his social criticism; indeed, the poetry has all too often been misread or neglected as merely statements in verse of his political and social persuasion. As Davidson's work has not been read by a large portion of contemporary readers, a good deal of summary has seemed necessary.

The first chapter is an account of Davidson's early life, the years in which he developed attitudes and convictions that shaped his artistic and professional career. Chapter 2 covers the years of his association with *The Fugitive* and the publication of his first verse, the period during which he was learning his craft—a time of experimentation when he was struggling to find the form best suited to his art and the subject matter with which to employ that form. Chapter 3 is concerned primarily with *The Tall Men,* Davidson's most ambitious poem and one in which the theme that recurs in much of his mature poetry first appears: the spiritual disorder and lack of purpose in modern civilization and society. In Chapter 4, the quality and content of his mature verse after *The Tall Men,* including his widely reprinted "Lee in the Mountains," is analyzed. The nature of Davidson's achievement as a prose stylist as he explores literary, social, and political ideas is scrutinized in Chapter 5. The ultimate aim of the entire study has been to suggest tentatively the nature and extent of his contribution to modern American literature, toward the time when his place among his contemporaries can be objectively determined.

DONALD DAVIDSON

Although we cannot record the full extent of our indebtedness, we wish to acknowledge some of the many who have been especially helpful in the preparation of this volume. We are grateful to the Research Council of Vanderbilt University and to Michigan State University for research grants which enabled us to do the research and to write this book. Several friends and colleagues read all or parts of the manuscript and offered many helpful suggestions; to all of them we are most grateful: John C. Coley, Joseph K. Davis, William W. Kelly, Virginia Rock and Floyd C. Watkins.

We also wish to express our appreciation to the late Mr. Donald Davidson for allowing us to use letters, manuscripts, and other items from his private papers, which are now deposited in the Joint University Libraries, Nashville, Tennessee; and to Mr. Allen Tate for permission to examine and quote from the Allen Tate Collection in the Firestone Library, Princeton University. Our greatest debt is to Davidson, who generously devoted many hours of his time to conferences and discussions of all kinds of matters essential to this study. Despite the invaluable assistance of all our many friends, however, the critical opinions and conclusions are our own and for them we take full responsibility.

THOMAS DANIEL YOUNG
M. THOMAS INGE

ACKNOWLEDGMENTS

The authors gratefully acknowledge permission of the following to quote from the indicated works:

Donald Davidson for quotations from *An Outland Piper,* 1924; *The Tall Men,* 1927; *Lee in the Mountains and Other Poems,* 1938; and *The Attack on Leviathan,* 1938.

Harper & Row, Publishers, for quotations from Twelve Southerners, *I'll Take My Stand,* Harper Torchbook Edition, 1962.

Holt, Rinehart and Winston, Inc., for quotations from Donald Davidson, *The Tennessee,* The Rivers of America Series, 1946 and 1948.

Louisiana State University Press for quotations from Louise Cowan, *The Fugitive Group,* 1959; and Donald Davidson, *Still Rebels, Still Yankees,* 1957.

University of Georgia Press, for quotations from Donald Davidson, *Southern Writers in the Modern World.* Lamar Memorial Lectures. Copyright 1958 by the University of Georgia Press. Reprinted by permission of the publisher.

University of Minnesota Press and Theresa Sherrer Davidson for quotations from Donald Davidson, *Poems, 1922-1961,* 1966.

Vanderbilt University Press for quotations from Donald Davidson, *The Long Street: Poems,* 1961; and *The Spyglass: Views and Reviews,* edited by John Tyree Fain, 1963.

CONTENTS

CHRONOLOGY

1893   Donald Grady Davidson, born in Campbellsville, Tennessee, on August 18; parents, William Bluford and Elma Wells Davidson.

1909   Graduated from Branham and Hughes School, Spring Hill, Tennessee; entered Vanderbilt University on "$100 loan and a little odd cash." Withdrew after one year because of lack of funds.

1910–   Taught in small Tennessee towns: Cedar Hill Institute
1914   (1910-12); Mooresville Training School (1912-14).

1914   Returned to Vanderbilt; in addition to college classes he taught at Wallace University School.

1916–   Taught at Massey School, Pulaski, Tennessee.
1917

1917   Entered Officer Candidate School, Fort Oglethorpe, Georgia, May 12; received bachelor's degree, *in absentia,* Vanderbilt University; commissioned Second Lieutenant of Infantry, August 15; assigned to 81st Division, Camp Jackson, South Carolina.

1918   Promoted to First Lieutenant. Married Theresa Sherrer of Oberlin, Ohio, June 8; in August, sailed for overseas duty with Company E, 324 Infantry, 81st Division; combat service in Vosges and Meuse-Argonne sectors.

1919   Daughter Mary Theresa born March 26. Left France for United States in June; discharged at Camp Sherman, Ohio, in July. Began teaching at Kentucky Wesleyan College in September.

1920   Worked entire summer as reporter, Nashville *Evening Tennessean.* Appointed instructor in English, Vanderbilt University; began graduate studies at Vanderbilt. Regular meetings of "Fugitive" group began.

1921   For summer employment, sold wall maps of Alabama and United States in the cotton-mill towns of Alabama.

1922   Received master's degree from Vanderbilt; on April 12 first issue of *The Fugitive* appeared.

1924   Promoted to assistant professor of English; began editing book page for Nashville *Tennessean*.

1924   *An Outland Piper.*

1925   Last issue of *The Fugitive* appeared in December.

1926   Won first prize in the South Carolina Poetry Society Contest for "Fire on Belmont Street."

1927   *The Tall Men.*

1928   Book page began appearing in Memphis *Commercial-Appeal* and Knoxville *Journal. Fugitives: An Anthology of Verse.*

1929   Promoted to associate professor.

1930   *I'll Take My Stand* (contributor); *Tennessean* book page discontinued.

1931   Began summer teaching as faculty member of Bread Loaf School of English, Middlebury College, Vermont.

1932–   After fire destroyed Wesley Hall, February, 1932, spent the
1933   following college year on leave at Marshallville, Georgia, the home of John Donald Wade.

1937   Promoted to professor of English; *Who Owns America?* (contributor); *British Poetry of the Eighteen-Nineties* (editor).

1938   *Lee in the Mountains and Other Poems, Including the Tall Men* (reissued, 1949). *The Attack on Leviathan: Regionalism and Nationalism in the United States* (reissued, 1962).

1939   *American Composition and Rhetoric* (reissued, 1943); Revised Edition with Ivar Lou Myhr in 1947; Third Edition in 1953; Fourth Edition in 1959; Concise Edition in 1964; Fifth Edition in 1968.

1942   *Readings for Composition from Prose Models* (in collaboration with Sidney Erwin Glenn); Second Edition, 1957.

1946   *The Tennessee: The Old River, Frontier to Secession* (Rivers of America Series)—illustrations by Theresa S. Davidson; awarded honorary degree, Cumberland University.

1948   *The Tennessee: The New River, Civil War to TVA* (Rivers of America Series); awarded honorary degree by Washington and Lee University.

1952   Collaborated, as librettist, with Charles F. Bryan, composer, in the writing and stage production of opera, *Singin' Billy.*

1955   *Twenty Lessons in Reading and Writing Prose;* state chairman, Tennessee Federation for Constitutional Government.

1957   *Still Rebels, Still Yankess and Other Essays.*

1958   *Southern Writers in the Modern World.* (Eugenia Dorothy Blount Lamar Memorial Lectures delivered at Mercer University, November 20 and 21, 1957.)

1961   *The Long Street.*

1963   *The Spyglass: Views and Reviews, 1924-1930* (book reviews and essays selected and edited by John Tyree Fain).

1964   Retired from teaching; became professor of English emeritus at Vanderbilt.

1966   *Poems: 1922-61*. Awarded honorary degree, Doctor of Humane Letters, by Middlebury College, Vermont. Edited, with Introduction, *Selected Essays of John Donald Wade*.

1968   Died in Nashville, Tennessee, April 25.

CHAPTER 1

The Man and the Land

I A Southern Frontier Family

T O TRACE the history of Donald Davidson's forebears is to describe the American frontier experience at its fullest. His great-great-grandfather, Andrew Davidson, of Scottish descent, came to America in the latter part of the eighteenth century and settled in southwestern Virginia in a cabin on the headwaters of the Clinch River. His progress in establishing a homestead and in rearing a family was interrupted by a tragedy commonplace to the advancement of the American frontier. Sometime during the 1780's, an Indian raiding party, probably Shawnee, moved into the territory to harass the settlers and steal horses. One of the Indian bands came to Andrew Davidson's home, where his family—his wife, three children, and two orphan children—resided; and Andrew returned home that day to find that the Indians had abducted the entire family.

According to one report, when the Indians arrived at their home beyond the Ohio, they tied the two little Davidson girls to a tree and shot them before Mrs. Davidson's eyes. Her boy was given over to the care of an Indian squaw, who accidentally permitted him to drown. The disposition of the orphan children was not recorded, but Mrs. Davidson was sold to a French trader living in Canada. With a persistence typical of the hardy frontiersman, Andrew sought his family as far northwest as the present Detroit. After two or three years, he found his wife in Canada and ransomed her from the Frenchman. She was brought home to Virginia, only to die shortly thereafter, evidently as a result of the privations of her terrible ordeal.[1]

Putting the total loss of one family behind him, Andrew moved westward around 1800-1805 into the settled Tennessee territory. He established a second homestead in Blue-Stocking Hollow, near Shelbyville, Tennessee, and married Sarah Muse. Here the family was to remain for several generations as it grew and prospered. One son, Isaac

S. Davidson, attained a reputation in his time as a successful physician and property owner, although he began with few financial or educational advantages.[2] Andrew's eldest son was Bluford Davidson, who married Susan White; their oldest son was Thomas Andrew Davidson, Donald Davidson's grandfather.

William Bluford Davidson, Donald's father, was born July 1, 1862, the oldest of nine children. Despite the economic difficulties of growing up during Reconstruction, he attained for himself a thorough education. He attended one of the earliest professional teacher-training schools, Holbrook Normal School at Lebanon, Ohio, where he received a bachelor's degree. After additional study at the normal schools at Winchester, Tennessee, and Troy, Alabama, "Will" Davidson (as his family and friends called him) became a schoolteacher. His first position was principal of the school at Mooresville, Tennessee, in 1891, where the music and elocution teacher was Elma Wells, a graduate of the excellent Haynes-McClean School at Lewisburg, Tennessee. Will Davidson and Elma Wells were married in 1892 and embarked together upon the roving existence characteristic of the rural schoolmaster of the period.

His next position was as principal in neighboring Giles County at Campbellsville, near Pulaski, Tennessee, where on August 18, 1893, their first child, Donald Grady, was born. The choice of his names, Davidson once recalled, was probably dictated by the genealogical past and the historic present: "When I was born, it was my mother, under my grandmother's influence I am sure, who gave me a Scottish first name—out of Jane Porter's *Scottish Chiefs,* no doubt. It was my father, a hopeful young school teacher, who chose for his son's middle name the name of the admirable Peacemaker—[Henry W.] Grady."[3] Four other children were born to the Davidsons—Thomas Heber, William Wallace, Rebecca Mar, and John Wells Davidson—while the family moved from village to town in Middle Tennessee.

II The Formative Years

Davidson's earliest memories were of Pulaski, Tennessee, where his father arrived in 1894 or 1895. The schoolhouse there was a handsome old Southern mansion, he recalled, and the Davidsons lived across the street from a family that raised peacocks, which paraded and called in the yard. One of the places Davidson remembered with the warmest affection was Lynnville, where around 1898 his father became co-principal of Lynnville Academy. The dignity of his father's calling, which entitled him, in those days, to the title of "professor," in no way separated Donald from the rest of the neighborhood boys. Like the rest of them, he dreamed of being a railroad man when he grew up, engaged in rough-and-tumble fist fights, and played baseball games with homemade balls. "Everybody was so *poor*," he recalled, "that we made our own baseballs out of hard rubber balls covered with twine."[4]

Of more importance to his later career as a writer were the casual boyhood associations with the remaining members of the generation who knew the Civil War by experience. His grandmother on his mother's side, for example, Rebecca Mar Patton Wells, was a rich source of fascinating first-person Civil War information. Her home was at Chapel Hill, Tennessee, where her family had been well acquainted with the Forrest family, kin of General Nathan Bedford Forrest. A widow, Grandmother Wells moved into the Davidson home early in Donald's childhood, and, since the household was crowded, he often slept in her room. She spent a good deal of time in the twilight hours recounting tales to Donald of her experiences during the federal occupation of middle Tennessee—experiences later recreated by him in poems included in *The Tall Men*.

One of Donald's great-uncles fought under Nathan Bedford Forrest, but was killed near Sparta, Tennessee. Another, in his early twenties, was captured at Fort Donelson and died in a Northern prison. A third was wounded at Murfreesboro and lay all night on the battlefield before medical aid arrived. Donald's mother had two uncles who rode with Forrest, and her father, after being invalided out of service, returned to Chapel Hill to operate his tailor shop and to make Confederate Army uniforms which had to be hidden whenever a party of federals came through town. During Christmas and other holidays, the Davidson home was often filled with visiting uncles who made tale-telling and joking the order of the day. "The old Confederate soldier was still a familiar figure in my early years, " Davidson wrote. "I have sat long hours with these old men, in the country store or by the fireside, and heard their tales."[5]

The most profound influence in his early years was his father, a man cultivated in both the formal disciplines of Classical knowledge and the informal heritage of regional tradition. The elder Davidson provided instruction in the Classical languages at home, when it was not available in the local schools. He read aloud a great deal to the children in the evenings, and young Donald was especially impressed with his reading from Bryant's translation of the *Iliad* and was also disturbed in particular over the treatment of Hector by the goddess Athena. The father often quoted, too, favorite passages from "The Vision of Sir Launfal" and "The Lady of the Lake," the first sentence of Johnson's *Rasselas,* and the opening lines of Shakespeare's *Richard III,* "Now is the winter of our discontent/Made glorious summer by this sun of York. . . ." He opened to his children's eyes, as well, the great wealth of native lore at his command by way of stories, folk songs, and ballads about the old times. Not until later in his life did Donald Davidson discover that these songs were of great interest to scholars and that his intimate acquaintance with them enabled him to make a contribution to the understanding of American and European folk culture, through both his writing and his teaching.

If Donald's father taught him the pleasures of native music, his mother was responsible for instilling in him a deep appreciation for classical music. A music and elocution teacher by profession, Elma Wells Davidson taught him to play the piano. Although he persisted in improving his proficiency, he did not practice faithfully enough to develop a technique; nevertheless, the influence of this early training had lasting effect. Throughout his life he was interested in understanding music as it related to composing. In fact, at one point in his later life, after a year's work at Vanderbilt University and several years of teaching, and after composing an original operetta, he seriously considered applying for admission to Harvard University to study music.

Another source of influence in Donald's home were the volumes that lined his father's bookshelves. In his father's copy of Dr. J. G. M. Ramsey's *The Annals of Tennessee to the End of the Eighteenth Century,* he read "Donelson's stirring account of his famous voyage down the Tennessee and various other narratives of notable deeds in Indian and pioneer times."[6] Available were copies of John Trotwood Moore's books, of which his father thought highly, such as *A Summer Hymnal* and *The Bishop of Cottontown,* and on the lighter side some of Opie Read's works. Davidson tackled Plutarch's *Lives,* the plays of Shakespeare, and the ninth edition of the *Encyclopaedia Britannica,* as well as all of the works of Cooper, Scott, and Poe he could find.[7] Longfellow's *Hiawatha* was among his early favorites, of which he memorized passages; and he read much of Byron, especially the narratives. But his father cautioned him against reading much of then popular sentimental European literature, such as prolific George Alfred Henty's adventure stories for boys, the sensational novels of psychic power and universal love by Marie Corelli (pen name for Mary Mackay), or the flamboyant romances of fashionable life written by Ouïda (pen name for Marie Louise de la Ramée), such as *Under Two Flags.*

Will Davidson did not believe that children should enter school until they were eight or nine years old. With the training he had already received at home, however, it is little wonder that young Davidson, upon entering Lynnville Academy in 1901, was placed immediately in the fifth grade. There he sat in classes under Miss Jenny Worley, who awarded him a fancy leatherbound copy of Longfellow's *Evangeline* as a prize for excellence in spelling. Later, he also had classes under his father.

His most exciting adventure in education came four years later when it was decided that he was to be enrolled at the well-known Branham and Hughes School at Spring Hill, Tennessee, at the extreme northeast corner of adjoining Maury County, almost thirty miles distant from his home. Although founded as recently as 1897, by 1905 Branham and Hughes had achieved a reputation as one of the most successful preparatory schools for boys in the South, through the expert guidance and supervision of founders William C. Branham and William Hughes.[8] This decision meant that Davidson would be living away from home at the tender age of twelve. But, for his first year, the family placed him under the care of his young uncle, Wallace Wade Wells, then a senior at the preparatory school. Wallace, only ten years older than Davidson, and the youngest brother of his mother, grew up with the Davidson family. He was like an older brother to his nephew, who regarded Wallace with a worshipful attitude throughout his boyhood; thus, nothing could have pleased Davidson more than the prospect of going to school with his Uncle Wallace at Branham and Hughes.

By the beginning of Donald's second year at the school, Will Davidson had left Lynnville and moved to Columbia, seat of Maury County, Tennessee, for a new position. For his second and third years, Davidson commuted by train, leaving early enough in the morning for a thirty-to-forty-minute train ride and a mile walk so as to arrive at eight o'clock. Uncle Wallace, who left Vanderbilt University after his first year, although he had made center on the varsity football team, came back to Spring Hill to enter the poultry business with William Hughes of the school, and then was joined by Grandmother Wells. For his fourth year, therefore, Davidson stayed with his grandmother and Uncle Wallace.

In the four sessions between 1905 and 1909, Davidson was exposed to a vigorous curriculum of standard classical courses— four years of

Latin, three of Greek—and to four of English and mathematics. From eight in the morning to three in the afternoon, he studied and recited Caesar, Homer, Euclid, history, and English grammar. By the senior year, the Branham and Hughes scholar was required to read the Greek hexameters of Homer's *Odyssey* aloud, in proper meter, scanning them at sight. The presence of a school paper at Branham and Hughes, *The Purple and White,* encouraged Davidson to make his earliest attempts at writing verse. He was also chosen, along with his classmate Horace T. Polk, to represent the Sam Davis Literary Society in the Commencement Debate with the Henry Grady Literary Society, the school's two literary clubs.

Polk and Davidson read through what was locally available of the *Congressional Record* in preparation for arguing the negative side of the question, "Should the U. S. Navy be increased for defense purposes?" and they won the debate. During his senior year, he earned a part of his tuition working as head spelling corrector. Immediately after the noon recess each day, all students took a spelling test that was written in uniform blank books. Student correctors marked the errors and reported them to Davidson, who kept the roll and recorded grades. He handed in a list of failures (those who missed three words out of the ten called out) for disciplinary action, which meant staying in for a half-hour after school was dismissed. Davidson was accustomed by then to helping earn his own way, having earned his first dollar from peanuts raised in his father's vegetable garden in Lynnville and from attempting as a boy to sell copies of *The Saturday Evening Post.* Of the last venture, he once reported, "at an early age I failed to exhibit any business ability, for I did not succeed—as other boys did—in selling *The Saturday Evening Post*; I refused, in fact, after some half-hearted attempts, to sell it at all. Thus, no doubt, I was saved from a business career."[9] The likelihood is, however, that there simply were not enough potential customers in Lynnville.

His practical experience, combined with his love of learning, served to convince the young scholar of the necessity for continuing his education. But the lack of financial resources for pursuing a college degree was a sizable problem, one which a fortunate conjunction of events temporarily resolved. In 1909, Davidson's father moved from Columbia to Bell Buckle to become principal of the high school there. Bell Buckle was the location of the nationally famous Webb School, a preparatory school for boys founded by "Old Sawney" Webb, the Tennessee schoolmaster who created one of the most distinctive educational programs in the South after the Civil War.[10] Will Davidson became acquainted with the older Sawney Webb, who learned of the younger Davidson's desire but inability to continue his education. The Boddie Loan Fund, which had been established at Vanderbilt University for Webb School graduates, had not been utilized for that autumn; and Webb offered to recommend young Davidson for the loan. The choice of schools could not have been better if planned, for once more Davidson was following in his beloved Uncle Wallace's footsteps.

III   University Days

In the fall of 1909, Davidson arrived on the Vanderbilt campus with the treasured letter of introduction which had to be personally authorized by Chancellor James H. Kirkland. Thus, he began his freshman year "on a $100 loan and a little odd cash," which was soon exhausted and required "further loans and more odd cash."[11] While his economic resources dwindled away, Davidson seized every opportunity to satisfy his intellectual thirst. In close proximity to a well-stocked library, he read through all of Kipling, some of Dostoevsky and Tolstoy, and various other writers suggested by his English teacher, Lawrence G. Painter, or by student friends. From schoolmates Ben and Varnell Tate, brothers of Allen who much later became a close friend, Davidson borrowed and read the complete works of de Maupassant.[12] But the year was all too quickly over, and there were no prospects of cash for continuing. Forced immediately to find a job at age seventeen, Davidson without hesitation chose teaching, a profession to which he dedicated most of the next fifty-four years.

Davidson spent the next four years in two small towns hoping to earn enough money to return to Vanderbilt, although his first salary amounted only to forty dollars a month. His first appointment from 1910 to 1912 to Cedar Hill Institute, at Cedar Hill, Tennessee, in the "black-tobacco" country came about because he was able, above all else, to teach Greek; but this was but one of a multitude of duties. "In those days," he once commented, "a teacher was expected to handle classes in English, Arithmetic, Plane and Solid Geometry, Greek, Latin, and perhaps History, all in a normal day's teaching schedule. . . . I leaped from bloody tragedies like Shakespeare's *Macbeth* to sentimental idylls like Storm's *Immensee* without undue discombobulation. It is a wonderful thing to be a young teacher and to have confidence in your powers."[13] In the afternoon he coached the boys at Cedar Hill in baseball and football and managed to find time to compose the words and music for a children's operetta based on the Pandora myth, which was performed first at Cedar Hill and later, when word got around about it, at several other middle Tennessee schools.

Cedar Hill was a fairly substantial town on the railroad in a tobacco-growing country, but Davidson's position for the next two years, 1912-14, was at Mooresville, a village off the railroad in a rich country of typical middle Tennessee "diversified" farms. It was at Mooresville twenty years earlier that Davidson's parents had met and married, so that part of the country had a special significance for him. The summers during these years while his family was still at Bell Buckle were spent in various ways to earn money—pitching hay on Sawney Webb's farm for a dollar a day; and, after the family moved to Mulberry, doing the same job on the farm of Bob Motlow, the brother of Lem Motlow, owner of the Jack Daniel distillery at nearby Lynchburg, Tennessee.

When Davidson finally managed to return to Vanderbilt in the fall of 1914, he was an immensely richer person in terms of maturity and practical experience; but his financial condition, still precarious, required that he take a job. Thus he taught classes in English and German at Wallace University School, one of Nashville's best private secondary institutions.[14] An unexpected assignment, he reported, was being put in charge of "a class of unruly small boys—all from the best Nashville families—to whom I was supposed to teach Biblical History."[15] He worked in his classes at Vanderbilt as best he could around his five-day-week schedule at Wallace, although he found it impossible to schedule the required course in physics which finally prevented his graduating with his class in 1916. By taking classes in the summer at nearby Peabody College, Davidson completed his degree in this two-year period at Vanderbilt, except for the physics course. During the summer of 1916, while taking a course at Peabody, he worked as a school-census taker in Nashville, and then accepted a position at Massey School in Pulaski for that fall.

During his busy second stay at Vanderbilt, Davidson did some reading and made some friends who shaped the course of his entire career. Never an ordinary Southern school, Vanderbilt had emerged during the first decade of the twentieth century as an institution distinguished for its liberal pursuit of academic excellence. Able to afford some of the country's outstanding scholars and teachers and to draw upon the graduates of a number of prominent Southern preparatory schools, no other institution would have been more likely to inspire in Davidson the intense spirit of imaginative and intellectual creativity he was to experience there.[16]

Under the chairmanship of Edwin Mims, a native of Arkansas and an already prominent expert in Southern letters and Victorian literature, the Vanderbilt English Department had added to its faculty several promising scholars. Among them was young Walter Clyde Curry, whose remarkably disciplined intellect allowed him to master and make contributions to an understanding of the three major figures of English literature—Chaucer, Shakespeare, and Milton. Davidson was enrolled in Curry's first Chaucer class at Vanderbilt, where he was already developing some of the ideas incorporated in his famous *Chaucer and the Medieval Sciences* (1926). Another influence was John Crowe Ransom, only five years Davidson's senior, a brilliant 1909 graduate of Vanderbilt and more recently recipient of a bachelor of arts degree in the literary humanities from Christ Church College, Oxford, as a Rhodes scholar.

Mims, Curry, and Ransom showed a personal interest in Davidson and inspired his love of things literary. "For me there was excitement in Dr. Mims' courses," Davidson recalled, "partly from the stunning revelation that English and American literature offered subjects to study, not just books to read." From Curry, in addition to what he derived from his courses, Davidson got, he said, "out of his own library, an informal reading course in modern European drama—Ibsen, Strindberg, Rostand, Hauptmann, Sudermann, and the like." [17] Under Ransom, Davidson as an undergraduate studied Shakespeare, but the slight difference in their ages and the similarity of their backgrounds—both were of rural Tennessee origin—soon led to a congenial intellectual association that was more personal than professional.

Another teacher who greatly impressed Davidson was Herbert Sanborn, professor of philosophy, whose classes he recalled with great clarity over forty years later: "One could but be awed and obedient when Dr. Sanborn strode vigorously to his desk, cloaked in all the Olympian majesty of Leipzig and Heidelberg, and, without a book or note before him, delivered a perfectly ordered lecture, freely sprinkled with quotations from the original Sanskrit, Greek, Latin, German, French, or Italian, which of course he would not insult us by translating." [18] Though Davidson was always somewhat "bookish," his classes under such creative teachers probably marked "the real beginning of my systematic devotion to literature." [19]

Another source of intellectual stimulation was some of the undergraduates Davidson came to know. One was young Canadian-born Alec Stevenson, whose father taught in the Vanderbilt School of Religion. Stevenson first led Davidson to discover the fiction of Joseph

Conrad, who became the subject of his master's thesis under John Crowe Ransom and of one of his earliest pieces of published criticism. Others were native Nashvillians William Yandell Elliott and Stanley Johnson, through whom Davidson came to know an eccentric and dominating Jewish mystic and writer, Sidney Mttron Hirsch. Drawing Ransom into their circle, Davidson, Stevenson, Elliott, and Johnson began to gather with Hirsch at Hirsch's father's apartment on occasional afternoons for what began as social but usually developed into lengthy philosophical and literary discussions.

Just turned twenty-one and but slightly acquainted with the schools of philosophy, Davidson recalls, "Like Stephen Dedalus in Joyce's *Portrait of the Artist* I felt myself destined to be but a shy guest at the feast of the world's great culture if the banquet were to consist of the categories of Kant and the heresies of Hegal."[20] Often Stanley Johnson engaged in a dogged and stubborn metaphysical debate with Ransom and Elliott, but a good deal of discussion, conducted with rhetorical questions in the pattern of a platonic dialogue, was devoted to a fantastic pursuit of symbolic and mystic word etymologies under the priestly and bizarre guidance of Hirsch. This secret knowledge, Hirsch assured the group, "was the wisdom of the ages—a palimpsest underlying all great poetry, all great art, all religion, in all eras, in all lands."[21] The younger men were sometimes amazed, seldom convinced, and often bored by the verbose Hirsch.

While Davidson had numerous other close friends among the students in the years 1914—16 and was a member of the Alpha Tau Omega fraternity, this group of young intellectuals was to prove especially important in his career. What none of them realized was that they were engaged in a dress rehearsal for a series of similar meetings four years and a world war later with the same principals and some additional persons, except that the subject then under discussion was poetry instead of philosophy; and the end result, instead of charming conversation, was the publication of a poetry magazine, *The Fugitive.* But the present group was not yet a literary association, as most of their writing was then purely collegiate.

Davidson had contributed during both his earlier and his later stays at Vanderbilt a few essays and poems to the student magazine *The Vanderbilt Observer,* none of which bears the sure stamp of Davidson the mature essayist and poet. Of the early poetic efforts, Louise Cowan has written that they are "without awareness of the inner nature of poetry. To him at the time, poetry was principally song, with no great burden of thought. Indeed, the close conjunction of poetry and music was always to be apparent in his work. When his keen logic was to couple with his urgent sense of history to give substance to his mature poems, they were still to have a structuralizing aural quality."[22] Only John Crowe Ransom got a serious start on his creative writing.

Davidson also recalled other pleasant activities, such as formal and informal musical sessions at the homes of faculty and friends; holiday excursions up the Cumberland River, often in the company of young lady friends; and visits to Nashville's Vendome Theatre, to see staged musicals and dramas—*The Merry Widow,* a Victor Herbert musical, Ibsen's *Ghosts,* Forbes-Robertson in *Hamlet,* Geraldine Farrar in *Madame Butterfly,* or Sousa's band conducted by Sousa. Afterward, there was a long walk back to the campus while Halley's comet blazed across the sky above Kissam Hall. "It was not exactly Bohemian," Davidson recalled, "nor was it anything like a Parisian salon; but it was not academic, either."[23] These pleasures were shortly to be interrupted by a series of saber-rattlings and aggressions abroad which finally led to a United States declaration of war against Germany on April 6, 1917. At that point, all thoughts of pedagogy and literature were set aside temporarily for the sake of "making the world safe for democracy."

IV War Remembered

Unknown to each other, Ransom at Vanderbilt and Davidson at Massey both applied for admission to Officers' Training School when war became imminent; both were accepted, and both were pleased to encounter each other at the training camp at Fort Oglethorpe, Georgia, in May, 1917. As had happened at Vanderbilt, Ransom confided in Davidson during free periods the results of his early pursuit of the muse: "Now in campaign hats and khaki, we sat in a grove of pines on the battlefield of Chickamauga, at the foot of Snodgrass Hill. Again Ransom drew a manuscript from his pocket. This time it was a large sheaf of poems. Under the pines he read me parts of what was published in 1919 as *Poems About God,* by Lieutenant John Crowe Ransom."[24] The training in military science Davidson was receiving proved immediately beneficial in that Vanderbilt permitted, through special provision, his work to substitute for the single course in physics needed for his bachelor's degree, which was awarded *in absentia* in 1917.

In August, 1917, Davidson received his commission as a second lieutenant and helped organize Company E, 324th Infantry of the 81st Division then being formed at Camp Jackson, South Carolina. Contingents of draftees began to arrive early in September from North

Carolina, South Carolina, Florida, and, later, from Tennessee and Alabama. Appointed as commander of the dominantly Southern division was Maj. Gen. Charles J. Bailey, a native of Pennsylvania and an 1880 graduate of West Point. Before General Bailey arrived from the Philippines on October 8, the officers were far along in training and disciplining the men for combat.

The division was moved to Camp Sevier, Greenville, South Carolina, in May, 1918, to replace the 30th Division then embarking for overseas. Such action made the prospects for the early arrival of overseas orders very likely. But, before the orders arrived, Davidson was married to a charming girl from Ohio whom he had met in 1916 in Pulaski where she was teaching Greek, Latin, and mathematics at Martin College. Since Davidson could not obtain leave, Theresa Sherrer came with her father to Greenville; and the couple was married on June 8, 1918, by the same Methodist minister (it so happened) who had married Davidson's father and mother.[25]

The 324th Infantry was ordered to Camp Mills, Long Island, in late July. Beginning July 30, the 81st Division was shipped abroad; and by August 16, 1918, it was assembled in France in the Tonnerre training area. Before final precombat training could be completed, the troops were pressed into action and moved to the St. Dié sector in the Vosges Mountains. Before they reached St. Dié on September 18, where they were to relieve the 92nd United States Division and join with the 20th French Division, the foot soldiers were moved by train to the Bruyères region. First casualties came when German airplanes bombed the troop trains before they reached the Bruyeres area. The lengthy sector that the division took over extended some fifteen miles from Lusse to Allencombe. Preparatory to entering the great Meuse-Argonne offensive, the division was moved to another sector and occupied a line equal in length to the first from Fort Douamont (northeast of Verdun) to Fresnes, with Davidson's 324th Infantry at the sought end.

On November 8, 1918, orders were sent from division headquarters at Somme Dieue, and received quite unexpectedly in the middle of the night, that an attack would be initiated against the Germans at eight o'clock on the morning of November 9. This hastily improvised "pursuit" was a part of the offensive movement ordered by Marshal Foch to intimidate the Germans while armistice negotiations were occurring. The two units to bear the initial impact were to be the 322nd Infantry and Davidson's 324th. Resistance was stiff; but, by that evening, the 322nd had captured Moranville while the 324th had fought a severe battle in the Manheuelle woods. Each unit suffered the loss of over two hundred men. Amidst occasional rumors of an impending armistice, other units continued the advance on November 10 with a heavy loss of men for every foot of ground gained.

While awaiting further orders, the 324th was relieved that evening by the 323rd Infantry and made a weary march by back roads to the north. The Germans kept up throughout the night a fairly constant fire of high explosives and gas shells, but division headquarters received word of the suspension of hostilities on the morning of November 11. The armistice went into effect at eleven o'clock in the morning while the 81st counted its casualties of about six weeks at the front: forty-three officers and nine hundred and eighty infantrymen. The 324th next moved on foot for a three-week trek to a billeting area in central France, near Châtillon-sur-Seine, where the unit was to await word of its return home, which would be slow in coming because of the division's low priority as late arrivals in France.[26]

It would be difficult to describe fully or adequately the impact of all these events on the mind and soul of young Lieutenant Davidson. Never having traveled before, he was suddenly transported to South Carolina and New York, then across the Atlantic on the Cunard ship *Aquitania* and through England to France. Among his fellow officers and soldiers, he made fascinating new friends of a sort quite different from his academic acquaintances; and, while stationed in France, he came to know some of the villagers quite well, especially in Dié and Belan-sur-Ource. The military life was radically different, of course, from anything he had known as a civilian. And the new responsibilities he had assumed as a married man before his departure also must have encouraged the development of a new maturity for which his former life as a romantic young student and teacher could hardly have prepared him.

Sometimes during his wartime experience, Davidson maintained a kind of contact with the stimulating friends and pleasant environment he had left behind by studying worn, typed copies of Ransom's early poems which he had carried with him to France. Although Davidson was not yet writing mature poetry himself, he was, under the creative influence of Ransom's efforts, trying his hand at it. During what leisure time he had while in France, he tried some experimental verse; and he wrote his wife for a copy of Amy Lowell's *Tendencies in Modern American Poetry* (1917), which she sent as soon as mail regulations permitted. Shortly after his return to the states, he wrote a sheaf of ten poems about his experiences for which Ransom later suggested the general title, "War Remembered in a Season of Tranquility." When

Davidson ventured to read some of them at a *Fugitive* meeting, they were coldly received. Davidson did prepare three typewritten copies of the poems as gifts for three of his closest army friends during the French campaign, [27] but the only poem of the group he has seen fit to publish is "The Roman Road at Dye," which appears in a slightly revised form in *The Long Street.*[28] Later on, Davidson used his experiences at the front artistically in a section of *The Tall Men*—"The Faring," one of the few attempts of American poets to write about World War I in verse, and a most effective and powerful verse narrative about combat during any period of time.

Davidson's thoughts in France, however, were about more immediate and personal concerns. While at the front, he had learned that Theresa was expecting a child. A fellow officer, S. Toof Brown, who knew of his family situation, has written, "It was hard to realize then the thoughts which must have been constantly in Don's mind and the agony which he must have suffered, particularly when at the front. Naturally, he spoke often of them, but his anxiety neither affected the performance of the job at hand nor did it reflect in his disposition."[29] While Davidson was awaiting news of demobilization after the armistice, his daughter Mary Theresa was born. He considered taking advantage of the opportunity that was extended to American soldiers to attend a French or English university during the spring of 1919, but he decided against it for fear that it might delay his return to the states.

Finally the long expected news of the return came on April 10, 1919, from General Pershing himself. The general arrived to review and inspect the troops of the 81st Division. As he walked between the ranks at a fast clip, Davidson was impressed with Pershing's distinguished military bearing and appearance. Following the inspection, the colors of the regiments were decorated with well-earned battle ribbons, and then the troops were massed to hear an address by Pershing. After expressing the gratitude of the American people for the division's valorous conduct in France, he announced that it was designated for a return to the states promptly. The soldiers cheered, not only because of this good news, but also because Pershing's remarks added a touch of spirited pride to their contribution to the victory of the American Expeditionary Forces. Two months later, the troop ships sailed for home; and the concluding lines of Davidson's "The Faring" succinctly express what must have been the silent thoughts of many another returning doughboy:

And now the tide ebbs west again. We are going
Home; we are homeward bound with music
Prouder than when we came and sad but rich
With memories of battle. We who were young
Are older now from death in a foreign land
Met and passed by. Remembering many comrades
We are coming home, fewer than once we were.
After the pilgrimage this is given to us,
Only to say we came with rifles once
Over the sea to a foreign battle, faced
The stranger's bullets, the cold rain, and worse;
Only to learn what only the soldier knows,
Men find their country beautiful afar.[30]

CHAPTER 2

Journey to Parnassus

I The Return to Nashville

WHEN LIEUTENANT Donald Davidson landed at Charleston in mid-June of 1919, he was eager to get to Oberlin, Ohio, to see his wife and his infant daughter; but he was not able to depart immediately. First, he had to endure a few days of necessary processing at Fort Jackson, South Carolina, before he was given preseparation leave. Then he decided to purchase a ticket that would allow him a brief visit to Nashville. With a wife and a young daughter to support, he knew he had to go to work immediately, and he wanted to discuss the possibility of an instructorship at Vanderbilt with Professor Edwin Mims, chairman of the English department. Too, he wanted to see any of his friends who might have returned to Nashville. While he was on active duty in France, he had relived those afternoons and evenings at the Hirsch apartment near the Vanderbilt campus and the long discussions that "ranged through poetry to philosophy."[1] Certainly, these were among the happiest and most memorable experiences of his life, but an even stronger magnet pulled him directly to Nashville. His interest in poetry, always strong, had been considerably strengthened while he was in the service; and John Crowe Ransom, Walter Clyde Curry, and others with whom he could share this interest were at Vanderbilt University in that city.

The visit to Nashville was in many respects a disappointment because hardly anyone was around—Ransom was not to return until the fall—and although Mims received him cordially (the two men had a long and pleasant conversation in the swing in front of Mims's home), there was no opening in the Vanderbilt English department. The last position had been given to William Yandell Elliott, who expected to teach while working on his master's degree. So Davidson went on to Oberlin to see his wife for the first time in over a year and to become acquainted with his daughter and with the members of his wife's family. Since finding a job as soon as possible was an absolute necessity, he began to look for a satisfactory situation in the Cleveland area.

The frustrations and anxieties of these months are reflected in *The Tall Men,* which Davidson wrote nearly ten years later. First, he went to a government agency designed to assist in relocating returning veterans, but no one seemed even slightly interested in his plight. He almost never attracted the attention of the office clerks, who were engaged in a "1919 version of the coffee break."[2] Then he filed applications with an advertising agency and with the Cleveland public schools, neither of which he ever heard from. After several other false leads that never developed into actual offers of employment, he sought and received an appointment with the managing editor of the Cleveland *Plain Dealer;* but he was told that, since he had no experience in journalism, he should come back after he had worked for a while on a smaller paper. Then, almost desperate, he received, through a Nashville teachers' agency, an appointment as chairman of the Department of English at Kentucky Wesleyan College at an annual salary of fifteen hundred dollars.

At Kentucky Wesleyan he was the only full-time member of the English department; and, during the 1919-20 session, he taught freshman composition, the survey of English literature, and advanced courses in Chaucer, Shakespeare, and American literature. Despite the small salary and the difficult teaching schedule, the year passed pleasantly. Davidson was happy to have his family with him in his own home for the first time, and his students, although not well prepared, were industrious and eager to learn. Even the library was adequate for his class assignments (he was surprised to find Skeat's edition of Chaucer), although not so satisfactory for his own reading interests.[3] Nevertheless, he had little trouble making up his mind when, in the late spring of 1920, Professor Mims offered him a position. Although the instructorship at Vanderbilt would pay only fourteen hundred dollars, Davidson would teach only eight hours;[4] therefore, he could begin work on his master's degree. Of almost equal importance was the fact that in Nashville he would have intellectual and literary companionship, the stimulation of which he badly missed in the small Kentucky college.

When Davidson returned to Nashville in June, 1920, after first leaving his wife and daughter in Oberlin until he could find an apartment, he found that the meetings of the Hirsch group had almost resumed their prewar pattern. As soon as Ransom had returned in the fall of 1919, he and Curry had resumed their visits with Sidney Hirsch, who was living with his brother-in-law, James M. Frank, at 3802

Whitland Avenue, about two miles from the campus. During that fall
and winter they were accompanied on many evenings by Elliott and by
William Frierson, a senior English major in the College of Arts and
Science. As soon as Davidson had secured summer employment on the
Evening Tennessean he began attending the meetings. Because he had
been trying his hand at poetry and was eager to learn more about his
craft, he was pleased to see that the discussions had changed so that
more attention was now given to literature, especially poetry, and less
to religion and philosophy.

The discussions soon became more and more concerned with the
specific problems involved in the composition of poetry. Davidson has
described the kind of meeting that finally developed:

First, we gave strict attention, from the beginning, to the *form* of
poetry. The very nature of our meetings facilitated and intensified such
attention and probably influenced Fugitive habits of composition.
Every poem was read aloud by the poet himself, while the members of
the group had before them typed copies of the poem. The reading
aloud might be followed by a murmur of compliments, but often
enough there was a period of ruminative silence before anyone said a
word. Then discussion began, and it was likely to be ruthless in its
exposure of any technical weakness as to rhyme, meter, imagery,
metaphor and was often minute in analysis of details. Praise for good
performance was rarely lacking, though some excellent poems might
find the group sharply divided in judgment. But even the best poems
might exhibit some imperfection in the first draft. It was understood
that our examination would be skeptical. A poem had to prove its
strength, if possible its perfection, in all its parts. The better the poem,
the greater the need for a perfect finish. Any inequality in technical
performance was sure to be detected. It was not enough for a poem to
be impressive in a general way. Poems that were merely pleasant, or
conventional, or mediocre did not attract much comment.[5]

It would be difficult indeed to estimate the importance of these
meetings, and the private conversations between members of the group,
to Davidson's development as a poet. At no other place in the country
in 1920, and in few other places at any time, could the young poet find
so many other talented, dedicated poets and critics willing to assist him
in perfecting his craft. The regularity of the meetings—they were
usually held on alternate Saturday evenings at nine—motivated the
novice poet to write, write, write, and to strive for constant
improvement. Davidson said that he felt as if he were going to class
unprepared unless he took one or two new poems with him to each
meeting, with a sufficient number of copies for the other "brethren";

consequently, unless the muse just would not respond, he was always ready with some new verses when his turn came to read. Although poetry was coming more and more to occupy a central position in his life, the stimulation of the Fugitive group—these frequent and regular meetings when he knew that his efforts would receive the closest critical attention of every one of its members—undoubtedly inspired Davidson not only to write more but to agonize more over every line he wrote than he would have done under less fortunate circumstances.

In November, 1921, the group added another member when Davidson invited Allen Tate, then an undergraduate and the younger brother of Ben and Varnell Tate with whom Davidson had been in school in 1909 and 1910, to go with him to the meeting one Saturday night. Neither Tate nor the group discussions were quite the same again;[6] for, as Tate twenty years later recalled his first meeting, "I cannot remember whether I felt any excitement except in my own vanity. For Don and John were professors; and when I got there the next Saturday night, being the only undergraduate present, I was flattered. Who read poems I do not know; yet I seem to remember that Don read a long romantic piece called 'The Valley of the Dragon' in which the monster shielded lovers from the world. I imitated it soon afterwards; but neither the original nor its echo was allowed to survive."[7]

Except for Sidney Hirsch, who "skittered elusively among imaginary etymologies, " the persons who most impressed Tate during these early meetings were Ransom and Davidson. "Don," he recalls, "was writing what I suppose were his first poems; they were about lovers and dragons, and there was one about a tiger-woman that I thought was remarkable; but Don's liking for this sort of thing declined at about the time mine did; and in the summer of 1922 he began to write poems that I think are among his best."[8] The shift in the nature of Davidson's verse to which Tate refers—from "Tiger-Woman" and "Following the Tiger" to such poems as "Corymba," "Dryad," and "Naiad"—was partially due to Tate's influence.

As Louise Cowan points out, Tate's compelling interest in modernism soon affected the entire group, especially Ransom and Davidson: "The exchange of energy between these three men was enormous, setting up an interior movement within the group, the direction of which was unnoticed by some of the members, resented by some, and immensely exciting to others. And it was at this turning point that the ones 'committed to poetry,' to use Tate's phrase, began to work with a new sense of power and importance."[9]

There were, of course, no deliberate and conscious attempts to exclude certain topics from the discussions, but nonliterary subjects were presented less and less. "We did not need to ask whether the Muse were thankless," Davidson recalls, "so long as we found excitement, week by week, year by year in strictly meditating, as indeed we did, the art of poetry. We meditated almost nothing else besides."[10] Everyone was so fully engaged in writing and revising his verse that he was little interested in "the price of cotton, the value of real estate, the industrialization of the South"; neither did he feel any compelling urge to explore the "state of religion or the state of science." A few years later, however, these and related topics were of grave concern to Davidson and some of the other Fugitives. During these early years "the pursuit of poetry as an art was the conclusion of the whole matter of living, learning, and being."[11]

II Fugitive Days

So avidly and successfully did they pursue the muse that by March, 1922, there was a sizable accumulation of manuscripts. At one of the regular meetings when Hirsch proposed that they publish a magazine, the other members of the group agreed and accepted Stevenson's suggestion that the publication be named *The Fugitive*.[12] Perhaps their decision to publish a magazine was influenced somewhat by the fact that Witter Bynner, during a visit a few months earlier, had indicated that "an audience could be found for a publication by the group."[13] Or maybe their courage to initiate such a perilous venture, one that required so much work and had so little chance of success, was bolstered by an awareness that their verse was as good as any appearing in the three important poetry journals founded in the South in 1921: *The Double Dealer* (New Orleans), *The Reviewer* (Richmond), and *The Lyric* (Norfolk).

Tate has said that, when the idea of a magazine was first suggested, he regarded the project as one "of the utmost temerity; if not of folly."[14] Davidson's response was somewhat different: "I could hardly believe, at first, that my *friends* really would go through with this bold undertaking. I thought it bold, indeed—but not folly. When all agreed that we would, we *must* publish a magazine, it was for me one of my moments of highest, undiluted joy—one of the few such moments of peculiar elation and, I could almost say, of triumph."[15]

Once the decision to publish was reached, the project was pushed forward rapidly. First the poems to be included in the first number were chosen by popular ballot, with Davidson keeping the tally on the back of an envelope containing a letter from Chancellor Kirkland notifying him that he was not to be assigned the faculty apartment for which he had applied. Of the poems considered only two received more votes than Davidson's "The Dragon Book."[16] After the contents of the magazine had been decided upon, the copy was taken to the most economical printer they could find because the cost of publication was defrayed by the members.

As little as Davidson could afford the financial expense,[17] he was even less able to spare the time such a venture required. Each member was supposed to obtain subscriptions and publicity, and all were to share in the editorial duties of makeup, proofreading, correspondence, and distribution. Even for a small journal of limited circulation issued four or six times a year, these duties were considerable; and no one in the group devoted more time and energy to the project than Davidson did, often to the detriment of his own work. Scattered comments in his letters to Tate show that he was aware of how much of his time and energy was being consumed by the routine but necessary details of publishing the magazine. Once, in a fit of pique, he wrote: "it seems to be taken for granted that I will meekly take all the burdens of Atlas on my shoulders, while the rest of the members here in Nashville are busily writing poems, writing novels, reading contemporary literature, and otherwise enjoying themselves."[18] And he commented on another occasion that the volume of correspondence "has increased about 1000%." Every day letters come from "far off places and I have answered them all."[19] Hardly any time was left for writing. "Instead of writing a poem for tomorrow night," he wrote on February 9, 1923, "I shall give an account to the Fugitives of how much time I've spent on their business, the major portion of the last four days." Anyone acquainted with the activities of the Fugitives and with the voluminous correspondence among the members of the group will readily agree with Randall Stewart's observation that Davidson was a major, not a minor, Fugitive and that perhaps more than any other member he was the cohesive force that held the group together.[20]

The choice of a name for the magazine, Tate has said, was a good one "because it invited ridicule."[21] This half-serious remark refers to the minor ripple of comment and inquiry which the title provoked despite Ransom's succinct explanation in the first issue of the magazine: *"The Fugitive* flees from nothing faster than from the high-caste Brahmins of the Old South."[22] Almost a year later, in a letter to Corra A. Harris of the Charlotte *Daily Observer,* on March 10, 1923, Davidson expanded the original statement: "If there is a significance in the title . . . it is perhaps in the sentiment of the editors (on this point I am sure we all agree) to flee from the extreme of conventionalism whether old or new. They hope to keep in touch with and to utilize in their work the best qualities of modern poetry, without at the same time casting aside as unworthy all that is established as good in the past." More than twenty years later he returned to this topic to insist he was not intimating that these youthful poets were detached from their society. Instead, Davidson insisted, they could assume that they "belonged in an existing, rather stable, society as persons if not as poets."[23]

To assess the total influence of Davidson's associations with the Fugitives and his experiences with the magazine on his artistic theories and on his poetry would be almost impossible. During the three and a half years of its existence the magazine carried, in addition to a brief critical essay and three book reviews, forty-eight of Davidson's poems—all of the poetry he published during this period except for thirteen pieces. Only fifteen of Davidson's poems published in *The Fugitive* have never been reprinted, either by Davidson in one of his collections or by an anthologist. Of the thirty-four poems included in his first book, *An Outland Piper* (1924), twenty-four had appeared in *The Fugitive*. It is obvious, then, that during its existence *The Fugitive*, as one would expect, received the bulk of Davidson's poetic output.

To Davidson, as to any young poet, the assurance that his conscientious efforts to improve his art would be given a sympathetic but thorough scrutiny by men of considerable critical talent must have motivated him to experiment, to try new forms, and, most of all, to continue his search for subject. He knew that the best of his poems, selected by a group of critics whose judgment he respected, would go out through the pages of *The Fugitive* to an audience which was highly selective though pitifully small. To the Fugitives, as Davidson wrote Laura Riding, literature was "a serious business." Since they had no wish to appeal to popular taste, they would not compromise their standards. *The Fugitive* would continue to publish only the best poetry its editors could find and to seek its readers "in the intelligent few everywhere in whom lies the real hope of American literature."[24]

The most important and lasting benefit to Davidson, in addition to some close and lifelong friendships, came from the intense analytical criticism that consumed a major portion of the group meetings. This candid evaluation of each member's poetic efforts carried over into informal conversations between meetings and in the frequent exchange of letters and manuscripts that occurred when some member was out of town and could not attend the meetings. Davidson has commented several times on the helpfulness of Tate's reactions to his individual poems.[25] And in his *Southern Writers in the Modern World* (1958) he reflects upon the general aims and purposes of the Fugitives and, by implication if not directly, upon the impact of their criticism upon his own poetry. The Fugitives, he writes, were from the first concerned "with what concessions should be made to experimentalism in the arts." Should one admit free verse as a valid form? (Some of Davidson's earliest verse was in this form; but he was probably discouraged from continuing in the medium because Alec Stevenson, to whom he showed the poems, was signally unimpressed.) Or, if one could not go as far as free verse, could rhyme *or* meter "be dispensed with, or, if not dispensed with, distorted?" How far could the poet go in trying new uses of diction and meter and still achieve the effect he desired? What license does the poet have with language?[26]

After many sessions of the most agitated discussion, Davidson wrote, the Fugitives agreed that the "formal element" in poetry was indispensable but that the English poets of the nineteenth century did not "offer sound examples of the application of the formal element." (Davidson's development is toward the formal and traditional, and his later poems are much less experimental than those he wrote in 1922 and 1923 while under the obvious influence of Tate and Ransom.) Consequently, they did not accept Wordsworth, Keats, Tennyson, Browning, and other poets of the nineteenth century as models of form or technique or as examples of subject matter; instead, the Fugitives turned in the early years to Shakespeare and Milton, and later to the "metaphysical" poets, and to Hardy and Yeats.[27] The "metaphysical" poets did not influence Davidson as much as they did some of the other members of the group. In the early 1930's he objected to their attempts "to make the short poem all inclusive, to squeeze 'epic magnitude' into short compass." Even in his most mature poems his approach is not one of indirection, and he does not strive for deliberate ambiguity.

The Fugitive poets could not accept the concept of the "pure poem," one devoid of emotional, intellectual or moral content; to them a poem must both "mean" and "be"—and Davidson's poetic development clearly reveals an increasing awareness of the artist's responsibility to communicate with his reader as precisely as possible. The Fugitives, he wrote, attempted to unite the "form of their poetry with the myth that ought to belong to it or, to use the sublime term, the religious concepts and symbols that alone can validate the merely literary concepts and symbols and establish them as poetry in a realm impregnable to the attack of skeptical science."[28] Davidson's poetry, at least from *The Tall Men* onward, is an attempt to unite "form" and "myth," a characteristic usually absent from the early verse because he had not then discovered the myth, the "religious concepts and symbols."

After the poet has "appropriated" a myth, he should attempt to treat it in a "detached ironic tone." Although irony is an important element in the tone of some of Davidson's best poetry, usually he is not "detached" from his subject in the way Ransom often is. Another characteristic of Fugitive poetry is the attempt to take a "thoroughly contemporary, even a commonplace subject and sublimate it by giving it a mythologizing or quasi-mythological treatment."[29] Davidson points out that this is the method of such poems as "Corymba," "Dryad," and "Naiad"—those which Allen Tate has called the "Pan series" and which, in his opinion, are among Davidson's best poems, though most readers would disagree.

In establishing close and lasting friendships, in giving a means of immediate publication, in providing the opportunity to develop poetic techniques and a theory of the purpose and function of poetry, and in allowing him, through continued effort and even through failure, to find his subject—in ways beyond exact definition—Davidson's associations with the Fugitive group and his experiences with *The Fugitive* are among the most important and influential upon his development as man and artist.

III   *An Outland Piper*

In December, 1925, when *The Fugitive* ceased publication, Davidson must have been satisfied, to some extent at least, with his accomplishments over the four and a half years since his return to Vanderbilt in the spring of 1920. Although he had taught almost a full load of freshman and sophomore courses, he had completed his master's degree in 1922; and, with his promotion to assistant professor in 1924, he had established himself as a tenured member of the English department. As literary editor of the Nashville *Tennessean,* a position which he had assumed on a part-time basis on February 4, 1924, he had well underway what John Tyree Fain has called "the best literary page ever published in the South."[30] And he had been, from the very first, an important and indispensable member of the small group of poet-critics who many years later would be proclaimed "the inaugurators of the Southern literary renaissance."[31]

But Davidson had during these years "meditated almost nothing else besides" the art of poetry, and he must have regarded these considerable accomplishments as below the rank of first importance. Nevertheless, he should not have been entirely dissatisfied with his achievements in this the most precarious and unpredictable of professions. Even allowing for the bias of a close friend, he had some reason to believe Allen Tate's encouraging report of June, 1924, that everyone he met in New York literary circles had "read and liked" Davidson. But Tate added, "they maintain you lack a structural sense," a comment which Davidson pondered over and reacted to in several letters during the next year or more. His poems, more than sixty of them, had appeared in nearly a dozen magazines of broad, if limited, circulation—journals surely read by "the intelligent few everywhere in whom lies the real hope of American literature."[32] In addition, several of his poems had been reprinted in the most widely read collections— headed by what was considered for years the standard index of contemporary verse, Louis Untermeyer's *Modern American Poetry*, and followed by William Stanley Braithwaite's *Anthology of Magazine Verse*, Stanley A. Coblentz's *Modern American Lyrics*, and Burton E. Stevenson's *The Home Book of Modern Verse*.[33]

Even more encouraging to the aspiring young poet, perhaps, was the appearance in 1924 of *An Outland Piper*, brought out by the Houghton-Mifflin Company. Although it was not reviewed as widely as Davidson undoubtedly wished, this collection received several appreciative notices. William Rose Benét wrote of it in the *Evening Post Literary Review*, John McClure in the *Double Dealer*, David Morton in *Bookman*, Harriet Monroe in *Poetry*, and Louis Untermeyer in the *Yale Review*. Unsigned reviews appeared in the *Nation* and the New York *Times Book Review*, as well as notices in many newspapers from various sections of the country. And the comment was favorable, though certainly not altogether adulatory. The poet was complimented for a "lively lyric gift" and a "nimble fearless mind," although it was hoped that the next volume of verse, of which "there should be many," would be a "little more unified and much less obscure."[34] Many reviewers thought some of the poetry derivative; the poets most often mentioned were Edward Arlington Robinson and T. S. Eliot. Although the comments covered a fairly broad range, they tended to center on such phrases as "sprightly, wistful, and serious,"[35] "graceful rhymes, with a light flicker of pathos";[36] "gentle cynicism";[37] "great charm" but marred by "fantastic lines";[38] "one of the few gifted lyricists of this country"; a "clear and distinct singing voice never off key";[39] and an "undisciplined but promising collection."[40]

The most favorable of the reviews was written by John McClure, editor of the *Double Dealer* in which several of the poems had first appeared. He opens with a statement that the Fugitive poets are the "most interesting in the South" and that Davidson "at his peak" is "probably the very best" of the Fugitives. He concludes with an assessment that brought an instant response from Allen Tate: "Such poetry is not written by many men. Its author is one of a select few in the United States. Passages in these poems seem to me to be among the finest in American verse."[41] From New York Tate wrote immediately: "I can't wait a moment to hail you with congratulations—and him, too, for that matter, for having sense enough to give you your due. . . . See what he says about Ye Fugitives! You bring honor to us all."[42]

But, as previously pointed out, Davidson's years on *The Fugitive* were a kind of apprenticeship, as they were with all the members of the group with the exception of Ransom who published in the magazine some of his best and most sophisticated poetry. For Davidson, it was a time of experimentation, of trying out various poetic forms and techniques and of searching for the subject that would release his developing poetic talent. To assess, then, the cumulative effect of this period of severe discipline, of "practice, criticism, and revision," one must examine closely the early poems of Davidson, in the order of their creation in so far as it can be determined, to see if there is a discernible process by which this dedicated young poet discovered not only the "myth" which was to be the subject matter of his most mature poetry but the literary forms in which he was to express his convictions and his feelings about this subject matter.

Comparison of many of these early poems as they first appeared in *The Fugitive* and other magazines with the versions included in *An Outland Piper* and in later collections reveals that Davidson revised his work thoroughly and conscientiously. He learned that a "somewhat coldblooded process of revision, after the first ardor of creation had subsided, would do no harm to art."[43] Most of the revisions show his increasing awareness of the poet's responsibility to communicate as clearly and exactly as possible, a development toward a direct and straightforward line, one less frequently interrupted by awkward and stilted expression and less dependent upon archaic and pedantic diction.

Davidson's first poems were about lovers and dragons, tigers and tiger-women. This choice of subject may reveal the poet's inclination to avoid some of the unpleasant aspects of the materialistic world in which he lived and to escape into an imaginative realm where lovers, singers, and others of acute sensibilities could be shielded from the harsh realities of an unsympathetic society. In the first year of *The Fugitive* he published five poems in this vein: "A Demon Brother," "The Dragon Book," "Following the Tiger," "The Valley of the Dragon," and "The Tiger Woman." A sixth, "John Darrow," which Davidson said was intended as an introduction to the group of Tiger poems, appeared in the first issue of 1923.[44]

"The Valley of the Dragon," the poem read by Davidson at the first meeting of the Fugitives which Allen Tate attended, is typical. Filled with images of "colored flies on honeyed errands," "golden sunsets," "silver moons," "thatch so kind . . . against the cold and rain," and "Love's low breathing," it is a romantic tale of an idyllic love that flourished in a land where the lovers are shielded "from the serpent-thoughts of men." But one night the "hushed rapture" is disturbed by the Dragon that comes "Sliding down the stars in fury." The lover cannot quiet his loved one's sobs; the spell is broken. The Dragon's "unholy breath set the dreaming valley aflame" and "all beauteous things were still at the dreadful clapping of his beak." Now the valley is full of smoke—the first appearance of smoke by which Davidson suggests destruction and the impurities of modern life, a symbol that frequently recurs in the later poetry. The lover asks, "Who will deliver me? I wander seeking a Charm,—/ A Spell, a Sword, a Faith beyond the strange sea's foam/ To smite and slay the Dragon-brood and rest in my fair home." As in the other poems in this group, the enemy is not identified; he is vicious, heartless, and completely destructive of any relationship formed on a basis not entirely materialistic. And the means of combating this unnamed monster are equally vague and indefinite; the charm which the lover seeks could include almost anything: "A Spell, a Sword, a Faith."

The Tiger poems follow the same pattern. John Darrow is enticed into the wilderness by a woman "with skin like cinnamon / And eyes bright black" riding on the back of a tiger. Although people try to persuade him not to follow the strange woman, saying "You must have magic / To follow on that track," he persists and, contrary to popular belief, Darrow is not destroyed:

> And yet no tiger ate him.
> He wandered back, men say,
> Another dreadful Lazarus
> Of calm unspeaking clay.
> Where Darrow walks, comes silence,

> The hush that strikes men cold,—
> The curse, the hope, the beauty
> That never must be told.

"The curse, the hope, the beauty / That never must be told" is certainly the aspect of the human predicament at which the poet is hinting in the other two Tiger poems included in *An Outland Piper*. [45] The Tiger-woman, in the poem of that title, beckoned from the jungle path when "dusk was close and men were dull" and the speaker followed "dreaming fanciful." He was not afraid to follow the tiger-woman into the dark jungle, for it was a "fearsome place" only for those who "hunt" and "slay." When they entered the forest, the tigers came "And fawned upon her breast in love"; he was not afraid, and "Upon their heads my hand I laid":

> And all the jungle things drew near,
> And all the leaves a music made,
> Like spirits chanting in a choir
> Along a bamboo colonnade.
> Too sweet for human harps to sound,
> It touched my blood; it fired my heart.
> The Tiger-Woman sang, and I
> Sang too, and understood her art.
> The moon rose up as never yet
> A moon of love had blessed the air.
> Oh, give my breast the Tiger's heart
> To tame me and to keep me there.

In these poems the poet's dissatisfaction with his predicament is evident, as is his desire to escape the restrictions of a materialistic world to find fulfillment in love and nature. "The curse, the hope, the beauty" can be found only outside the patterns of "civilized" living. This theme is most clearly expressed in "Following the Tiger," in which the speaker prepares to follow the "track of the Tiger/ Into the thick of the wood" by first disposing of his worldly possessions. He grows weary of toiling, puts on a beggar's clothes, borrows "a lute of the tinker," and places a rose in his cap. The reason for the journey is unmistakable:

> For the feet of the Tiger pass
> Where no man ever has trod.
> The lair of the Tiger is blessed.
> Its place is the place of God.

In the wilds of nature, his only possessions being his rose and lute, he finds a place uncontaminated by the evils of man. Following the sound of a "sweet bell," he comes upon "A chimney, a smoke, a spark" and realizes he has found "the long-lost Queen of the Faëries." When she "loosened her hair," she "shook out a million stars," and the speaker thinks:

> *Oh, the claws of the Tiger*
> *Are sheathed, and the Peace of God*
> *Rests on this house, and beauty*
> *Walks where the Tiger has Trod.*

Then the door opens, and the speaker discovers a holy trinity:

> There were the lovely three,—
> God, and the Queen, and the Tiger,
> And God's hand welcomed me.
> The Tiger slept on the hearthstone.
> The Faëry gave me her ring.
> My rose began to blossom;
> My lute began to sing.
> *It sang how the ways of the Tiger*
> *Led me to beauty and God,*
> *To the door of the hut of the Faëry*
> *By paths men never have trod.*

Because the speaker has followed the tiger into nature, away from a world intent upon getting and spending, his rose blooms and his lute begins to play. Both images suggest that the creative impulse can flourish only when the artist removes himself from the stultifying demands of an unsympathetic society. Like the rich man in Matthew, man must give up his desire for the world's goods if he is to realize fully his highest potential. In 1922 and 1923 Davidson, along with many others of his generation, was evidently pondering the fate of the artist in a society in which he was not particularly welcomed.

Two other poems written in the early 1920's and collected in the first section of *An Outland Piper* reveal the poet's dissatisfaction, a rather indefinitely stated feeling of loss in the modern world. The first of these poems is "A Demon Brother," which was published in the first issue of *The Fugitive* and which, with major alterations, became the title poem of *An Outland Piper.*[46] In a letter written to Tate on July 25, 1922, Davidson indicated the essential situation presented in the poem: "The Demon Brother heard pipes when he was young and was filled with a burning desire to learn the secret which kept eluding him." The Demon Brother was surprised to learn how much like him the piper was: "His brow, his gesture even his dress" were "Perfections" of his "awkwardness." He followed the piper, and the music changed everything: "Streets tipped, I thought, in ravishment." The piper, who is not appreciated by the mob, advised the youth not to follow him, "Though I be of your father bred," because "You'll find the walking world a cheat." Despite the piper's advice, the young man could not help following him; and the results, though expected, are not altogether happy: "his piping sweet" has left the young man to know "the world's deceit."

The songs of the outland piper, then, have the same allurement as the track of the tiger and "the hope" and "the beauty" that enticed John Darrow into the forest. In addition to a crude kind of lyric symbolism, these first poems are seminal in that they introduce a basic theme found in much of the later poetry: a profound sense of loss in the modern world. The method, however changes: the approach becomes more direct and expository; the style, less lyrical; the rhythm, less regular; and the imagery, less romantic. Certainly these poems do constitute more than "a symbolic flight" from reality (the phrase is John L. Stewart's[47]); they are the first vague and incomplete statements of a theme which appears in much of Davidson's later poetry, the search for a rightful heritage, and which is fully developed for the first time in *The Tall Men.*

With the possible exception of the title poem, "Old Harp" is the most successful piece in the first section of *An Outland Piper.* Davidson said this poem was the result of an image which first occurred to him while he was in Walter Clyde Curry's Anglo-Saxon class:[48] a harp has been deposited in a museum with a small descriptive card. The poet imagines the "shame and hurt surprise" that the harp's former owner would feel if he could rise "From his dark mound by the sea" and view his instrument "placarded" here. With this harp, its owner once had sung "In tongues men have forgot" of "sleeping barrowed kings," "shield-rimmed galleys," "viking eyes ablaze," and "blue cliffs slowly rifting/ That guard enchanted Bays":

> But his pliant hand is dust
> Here is no singing tongue.
> Only the mute cool rust
> Fingers thee, loosely strung,
> And men read, as read they must,
> What once was sung.

Again Davidson is expressing his longing for something which man once possessed but which now seems forever lost. This time, in rhythm appropriately elegiac, he laments the loss of the great songs, the passing of the lyric and folk tradition. And it is a loss that society can ill afford. The proper place for the artist, he writes in "A Mirror for Artists," is among his people.[49] Great art, he argues, "has rarely been purely aristocratic. It has generally been also popular art in a good sense and has been widely diffused."[50] His most eloquent statement of this position was made in an address given nearly twenty-five years after "Old Harp" was composed: "A poetry that puts itself in a position not to be recited, not to be sung, hardly ever to be read aloud from the pages where it stands, and almost never to be memorized, is reaching the danger edge of absurdity."[51] For poetry, he continues, this development is a kind of "death-in-life, to exist only on the printed page, not on the lips of men, not to be carried by their voices and therefore almost never carried in their memories, rarely in their hearts."[52] The muted harp carefully placarded and placed in a museum, an "art object" completely removed from the function for which it was intended, is, for Davidson, indicative of what can happen. Poetry, he thinks, is doomed unless a way can be found to restore its oral character: "But that is a problem for our civilization no less than for our poetry. . . . No civilization of the past has ever lived without poetry. Our civilization can hardly be an exception."[53]

This sentiment expressed in "Old Harp," like that in so much of his early verse, suggests an insight that later developed into a firm conviction. An underlying theme in many of these early poems is the thinness of the present contrasted with the richness of the past. Here the poet laments the decline of poetry, its disappearance as a vital force in the lives of a people; later these views led him to pointed arguments in defense of traditionalism.

The second section of *An Outland Piper* contains much of the poetry that Davidson began writing in the summer of 1922 when he was consciously experimenting with form. On July 24, 1922, he wrote Allen Tate that he was attempting to capture the "elusive something you are always getting into your poems." Davidson's chief fault, he wrote, "is largely in restraint" and in "saying the pat obvious thing." Although he does not stray far from his usual stanza of four or six rhymed pentameter or tetrameter lines, he obviously tries to tighten his diction and to heighten the sardonic tone of the verse. The poems are less lyrical, the imagery less romantic, and the irony more pervasive.

In his *Southern Writers in the Modern World*, written twenty-five years later, Davidson describes the kind of verse he was trying to write during the latter part of 1922 and the early part of 1923. Although he is referring to the effect of the severe criticism that each of the Fugitives received from other members of the group, his remarks seem particularly applicable to his own experimentation: ". . . severe discipline made us self-conscious craftsmen, abhorring looseness of expression, perfectly aware that a somewhat coldblooded process of revision, after the first ardor of creation had subsided, would do no harm to art. It also led to what we sometimes called a 'packed' line. The poet, anxious to fortify his verses against criticism, strove to weed out anything 'loose.' This 'tightening up' might produce a poetry far less fluent and easy than was the current fashion."[54] The best poetry in the second section of *An Outland Piper* contains what Davidson calls the "packed line." The poet is not striving in these poems for simplicity of execution: his approach is indirect; his intentions more deliberately modern; his tone more consciously ironical.[55]

The best poems in the second section of the book are "Corymba," "Dryad," "Naiad," and "Avalon"—the ones Tate called "the Pan series."[56] In all of these poems Davidson is attempting to combine a "certain satiric touch," a "hardness of texture" with "lyrical beauty."[57] All of them are based on a theme of protest, and they employ an ironic and sometimes sarcastic tone. The rather esoteric mythology of "The Tiger-Woman," "John Darrow," and "Following the Tiger" does not dominate these poems, as it did many of the earlier ones; but around them there does hover a vague, unidentifiable supernaturalism.

Many years after the fact, Davidson indicated his dissatisfaction with his "Tiger" and "Dragon" poems and suggested his reasons for altering his poetic stance. One of the things he and some of the other Fugitives were attempting to do, he wrote in *Southern Writers in the Modern World,* was "to take a thoroughly contemporary, even a commonplace, subject and sublimate it by giving it a mythologizing or quasi-mythological treatment." His poems about dragons, tigers, and tiger-ladies were attempts at this "mythologizing or quasi-mythological" treatment; but they did not "come off" because the basis of the myth was too personal and esoteric, the treatment too directly romantic:

I found that if I used an old-fashioned dragon, in some perfectly direct romantic way, as an image of great danger and evil, the poem did not "come off." But if, using entirely contemporary language, I could think of a flapper of the nineteen-twenties as a reincarnation of a temple dancing girl of some remote century, the result might be such a poem as "Corymba." I do not think well of that poem now, but it was the first poem of mine, I believe, that won warm praise from Allen Tate. It conformed, I suppose, to the principle that he set forth in his April, 1924, Fugitive article as to Baudelaire's theory of correspondences: "that an idea out of one class of experience may be dressed up in the vocabulary of another."[58]

Whether "Corymba" is the first of Davidson's poems that "won" Tate's "warm praise" cannot, of course, be determined; but Tate's reaction to it was enthusiastic. Across the top of the manuscript copy which Davidson sent him for his comments, Tate wrote: "The best poem you have ever written, and I should also say the *best done by any Fugitive* in the past year." The other marginal comments amply demonstrate the close attention the two poets gave to each other's work. Although Tate objects to Davidson's use of certain words—"pale," "jaded," and "gaudy" ("Fact, that's all. What about your reality stuff?")—he encircles "plasm" in the line "Does her plasm breed toxin/ From phonic ecstasies!" and exclaims "Et tu, Brute! Yea, Bo!" Beside the following stanza Tate notes: "Considered in its context, this is the best stanza you've written all summer":

> Who shall say in mockery?
> "Cheeks were too hotly flushed!"
> Or that knee still touched too closely
> After the drum was hushed!
> Over her eyes certain
> And trance-like beauty was brushed.

After the last two lines, Tate writes: "The best two lines you've ever penned."[59]

This poem is one of the best examples in *An Outland Piper* of the poet's attempt to have his language draw simultaneously upon the senses and the intellect—to present the poetic experience, not to state it. Corymba's yellow hair bears no snood to indicate her unmarried state, but it is just as well because the "pale youths" are looking elsewhere. She has gone with a "jaded youth" to a "sudatorium" where the "sweating" is of movement "To a cacophonic drum. /The bodies flex, the arms twine/ In rhythmic delirium." In this situation, then, Corymba is seen in her natural habitat, a daring flapper of the 1920's. Although the imagery through which the poet presents the young girl and her surroundings is obviously erotic—"sleek curves," "flesh powdered and bare," "arms lifted," "bosom bared," "bodies flex," "arms twine/ In rhythmic delirium"—the tone of the poem is one of sterility. With her "drawn-up knees" Corymba has not rejected "familiarities"; she dozes and thinks of "new stockings" and "other such verities." Her physical beauty is not susceptible of "Isis' warm commune"; she will not practice her beauty before it fails—to paraphrase Ransom's advice to his Blue Girls (before "The priests come,/ and Shava breathes on clay")—because, like the women in T.S. Eliot's "The Love Song of J. Alfred Prufrock," her interests are elsewhere, as well they might be since the youth, her companion at the sudatorium, is "pale" and "jaded." Although the poem contains no direct statement of the poet's intentions, its tone, through which his attitude may be surmised, is unmistakable. The world of Corymba and her friends is sterile, without purpose or direction; and its inhabitants are frivolous and impotent.

Other aspects of modernity receive the poet's attention in "Dryad" and "Twilight Excursion." In the first of these the irony of the title is perhaps too obvious. A dryad—in Classical mythology, a nymph presiding over woods and trees—is given an ironic, twentieth-century treatment. The hopes of this modern nymph, the "city's straitened acolyte" whose "heart went hungering on the winds," are "mured at the gingham counter." In this unfulfilled condition, "Her loveliness, kept still unspent," she is enticed into the woods by the "delirious satyrs' laughter" of a slim youth. Although she sees the "faun's ears in his hair" and the goat's legs underneath his suit, when he "came beckoning;/ Her prancing senses drew her after." The poem concludes with a succinct statement of her "profits and losses":

> She found? What cities could not give,
> Bare beauty by a careless pool.
> She lost? That is for reasoners
> And titillators of the School.[60]

In "Twilight Excursion" (the twilight is "warm as a woman's flesh") a man flees from the frustrating atmosphere of his uncreative world. The "fragmentary sight of men" could not tell he was fleeing, bolting from the sterility of "the pits of livelihood." They do not know that "out of the wood—/ A satyr" stamped a "cloven Hoof," and a "summoning drum . . . kept beating." So man is drawn away from the materialistic world in which he lives, but to what?

> And here, a dark vine scented the stair.
> What was he groping for there in the dusk?
> Not a bell—but a bush for the hand to cleave!
> Not a door—but a slough of the garment's husk!

> The lordly buildings drooped to grotesque.
> There was stench in the pits of livelihood.
> But the summoning drum in the wood kept beating
> As she came, with lips of flesh and blood.
>
> Then a table's white and silver kept
> The passion of a renegade,
> Considering, to a muted drum,
> The tainted posturings of a maid.

The same general subject matter is used in "Naiad," and the detached manner of presentation is maintained. But the ironic attitude, the obvious and often abortive attempts at witticism, and the rather heavyhanded sarcasm are largely missing; instead, there is an attempt to create an atmosphere of a "vague, hovering supernaturalism."[61] In a letter to Tate, written July 25, 1922, Davidson summarized the contents of the poem: "A young girl, very beautiful of body, is bathing in a river with a group of companions—men and women in the tawdry attire which custom imposes. She slips away to a place beyond the bend in the river, strips off her bathing suit, and goes in the water alone":

> Dripping, she stood, and madness stung her blood,
> And strange desire unsheathed her tender breast.
> All ancient beauty sang upon the flood,
> And she made her beauty naked for that behest.

The third line in that stanze, Davidson writes, is "intended to wake the spirit of wonder, a statement of the vague and indefinite forces which impelled this modern girl to go naked into the river. From this standpoint the line is couched in a significant symbolic form, the atmosphere of the poem is lifted just that much more into the realm of the ultra modern."

Relieved of the bathing suit, her last connection with the world of men and its restraining customs, the young girl submerges herself in the river. The language of the poem suggests that the union is both sexual and spiritual:

> The skittering dragon—flies beheld her lust,
> And her plunging whiteness deep in the green deflected.
> The penumbral depth received her slim trunk's thrust,
> Like lover gesturing, "Come, O Long-Expected!"

But then something happens to her; exactly what the poet leaves deliberately ambiguous. Perhaps she is dragged down by the river-god, for the moment of her last descent is one of spiritual union; like the protagonist in Hemingway's "The Short Happy Life of Francis Macomber," an instant is her life, the moment when her lust becomes love and the union with her lover one of purest spiritual exstasy:

> A warm hand glided across her passioned breast.
> A seeking arm clutched her in the abyss.
> She saw the urgent eyes, the God's hair cressed
> With flowering slips, and yielded to his kiss.

She is finished with the world, but it is not finished with her, for the girl's naked body is discovered by a member of a searching party:

> The fat and lean beset the dark with light,
> And searching voices frittered to and fro.
> A rustic, stumbling in a sandy bight,
> Gloated upon the dead with obscene woe.

With the exception of the title poem and "Old Harp," the poems in the Pan series are the most successful in the book. Although Davidson was yet to find the subject that would enlist his considerable poetic talent, his medium in these poems is carefully controlled. The excesses of imagery and diction, characteristic of the earlier poems, are, for the most part, excluded. There are no more dragons, tigers, and tiger-ladies. Because of the tentative and experimental nature of the poems, some of the verses do not quite ring true; the artist is carefully learning his craft, preparing for the time when he will come upon the subject demanding all of his skill.

Except for "The Wolf," the remaining poems in section two and those of section three are the least satisfying in the collection. Many of these poems treat various derogatory aspects of the American materialistic civilization, and they tend toward despair and cynicism. Their unity of tone is often disturbed by a pertness and by an attempt to shock.

"Redivivus," a weak poem but the one which Harriet Monroe, for some strange reason, chose to quote in her review, presents the less-than-novel idea that an instrument often gives out an unexpected sound. Since "the probing knife of madness/ Can start a dullard brain" and "the surly heart of clown/ Can crack with ecstasy," the poet requests:

> Then let my skeleton soul
> Write upward from the loam,
> Drink red morning again,
> And look gently home.

But neither this poem nor "Requiescat," which is imbued with the skepticism popular at the time, suggests where home is. The supernatural world may be as empty and purposeless as the phenomenal one, for no benevolent being or force seems to be guiding the destiny of the insect or, one would suppose, of man. Spurned by the wheel of fortune, the caterpillar lies dead, "done/With his last journeying." Its aspirations, past experiences, promises or hopes matter not; the dream of life is over:

> The cosmos has used him
> In its blunderings.
> The senseless wheel has bruised him.
> Wheels will do such things.

The short line and lilting meter, as well as the turn of the last line, seem to indicate that the poet is not entirely serious. The subtitle, "Pathetic Fallacy," and the poet's incongruous use of subject and language suggest that his intention is satirical or that he is striving for the effect that Ransom derives from such incongruities as "transmogrifying bee." Perhaps this obscurity of purpose makes the piece little more than an interesting poetic exercise: it demonstrates the scope of Davidson's experimentation.

But the poet seems more at home in such poems as "Voice of the Dust" and "The Wolf" in which his approach to his subject is neither oblique nor ambiguous. In the first of these the absurdity of man's vanity is clearly and directly stated; his boasts of accomplishment are hushed by the "dry rasp in the beat of the wind":

> What marvels man has made! What art!
> "What fury tamed!" the voices said.
> "What wonder is the human heart!
> "What miracle the human head!"

These boasts come from all parts of the world; so many and so persistent are they that "continents hummed with the sound" and "seas crashed with reverberant foam." But finally a whisper is stirred out of the dust:

> At last the sodden dust bestirred
> Whispers that were not soft or kind,
> And in all space no sound was heard
> But a dry rasp in the beat of the wind.

The most successful of the poems concerned with the fallibilities of man is "The Wolf." Set in a country store, it employs the kind of material that Davidson later used; and, like "Corymba," it shows the poet experimenting with the theory of correspondences. According to this theory, "an idea out of one class of experience may be dressed up in the vocabulary of another." Using the language and imagery naturally associated with the country storekeeper in his usual surroundings, Davidson succeeds in presenting convincingly man's animalistic nature, his blood-sucking rapaciousness. In this context, the man becomes a wolf. The poem succeeds because of its language: simple and concrete, it appeals simultaneously to the senses and the intellect. Blending perfectly with the subject matter of the poem and its tone of high seriousness, the language succeeds in presenting, not stating, the poetic object:

The Wolf

The flour-barrels, cracker-boxes, cans
Of lard and coffee hem the live beast in,
Who jingles furtive fingers through the till,
Dropping delicious coins with snap and grin.

Drooling, like who should be crunching bones,
He mouths the figured column of his kill.
A sneaking blast rattles the locked door;
The cat looks on, oracular and still.

The eyes that should be centering the brush
Blink at the hot stove's belly, glowing red.
The breath that should go howling to the moon
Blows out the lamp and wheezes off to bed.

To those who know of the unscrupulous practices of many Southern country storekeepers in the tragic period following the Civil War, Davidson's choice of subject for this devastating treatment appears deliberate. That the poet thinks well of this poem is indicated by the fact that it is one of the five poems from *An Outland Piper* included in *Poems 1922-1961.*[62]

Davidson's other satires on various aspects of twentieth-century life are much less successful than "The Wolf." They reveal an indecisiveness about poetic technique and, perhaps, a lack of conviction in what he is trying to do. His attitude toward these pieces is clearly indicated in a letter to Tate, in which he included "Ecclesiasticus II" for his friend's comments.[63] He knows he is "treading" on Tate's "preserve," but, he writes, "I think it is much easier to write this kind of thing, and for that reason I am a little inclined to doubt the artistic sincerity of those who affect this style, including you and myself both!" A brief look at three poems gives, perhaps, an adequate indication of Davidson's experiments with bitter satire. All three have the same mocking satiric tone, which at times verges upon sarcasm, the same attempted witticisms, and the same pertness of diction. In "Ecclesiasticus I" the poet assails false religiosity in the cleric who ignores the natural laws of good gardening:

> I saw Ecclesiasticus
> Shelling a pod of a wind-dried pea.
> The little seeds would grow, he said,
> If only he planted them prayerfully.

After the gardeners had prepared the soil, Ecclesiasticus "asked the blessing of the Lord" and "vowed the saints on high rejoices." When the rain and sun caused the peas to sprout and grow, Ecclesiasticus could not be bothered to care for them because from his comfortable seat in the shade, he was writing "emendations on The Word." But, when the plants flourished, he took full credit, calling this development "the harvest of Thy servant's toil" and ignoring the careful efforts of the gardeners. When the insects began to destroy the plants, Ecclesiasticus, who did not allow the gardeners to apply poison, called the catastrophe an example of God's Providence. The bases of the satire are clear: false religiosity, pompousness, stupidity (the cleric does not understand how he can best serve God), and faith bordering on superstition. But the minister's gravest sin is selfishness. When the harvest fails and there are few peas for the table, Ecclesiasticus is not concerned because "he had roasted chicken/ And thanked the mercy of the Lord." If his harvest should be slight—that is, if he should fail in his purpose of bringing souls to God—he will not worry because in his egoism he believes *his* salvation is secure. Through His infinite mercy, God has elected to save him.

The cleric portrayed in "Ecclesiasticus II" is of a different sort; but, like his counterpart, he is completely oblivious of his duties and functions:

> Pronounceth dread epiphany
> At every membership's increasing;
> Acclaimeth Jack's sobriety
> Upon Jack's drunkenly deceasing.

This social-minded minister sanctifies Boosters' Clubs, attends forty teas a week, finds bare flesh satanical, and powder-puffs abominable,

> Pointeth a way to Zion's gate
> Via 100% Americanism;

Photographs God in pants
Expectorating on Bolshevism.

While he is dissipating his energies on trivialities and knocking down
"straw men of monkey origin," only Christ "walks and weeps" with the
"sinful multitude."

The "Iconoclast" centers upon another tendency of the time. In an
acceptably fashionable manner, the iconoclast raved at the "ugliness of
matters," upset "formulated god heads," punctured credos, and
arranged "human idiocies in columns." For his diatribes he became
famous, was offered state decorations, and was plagued by lucrative
offers for speeches. Yet a "shadow always goaded him"; he could never
find the thing he sought. As his books became famous and "Mobs in a
thousand cities stormed the shops/ To change their silver for his new
edition," the cause for his discomfiture is revealed: "He glowered at a
manuscript and gnawed/ A pencil,—and loathed his personal situation."

The fourth section of *An Outland Piper* is composed of a single
poem—"The Man Who Would Not Die." The longest piece in the book,
114 blank-verse lines, it, along with "The Swinging Bridge" and
"Legend in Bronze," is most indicative of the subject matter and the
manner of Davidson's mature poetry. The three poems anticipate
Davidson's characteristic tone and mature style, first found in *The Tall
Men*. The tone, particularly of "The Man Who Would Not Die," is
sardonic rather than cynical. The blank verse, though conversational, is
precisely phrased, looking toward the dignified, clear, and smooth, but
not swinging, line of the mature poetry. His experimentation with the
ballad stanza and with tetrameter and pentameter quatrains that is
characteristic of much of his early verse is almost finished. He is moving
toward the blank-verse line as the medium that gives greatest freedom
to his narrative and descriptive abilities.

"The Swinging Bridge" is perhaps the earliest poem clearly to
suggest the later manner. The line flows smoothly but not too easily;
the diction is simple, concrete, and evocative. The romantic imagery of
the earlier poems is missing, as is the esoteric, archaic, and learned
vocabulary. The tone is dignified, the approach certain and direct.

> The Swinging Bridge
> Not arching up, as some good bridges do,
> Nor glum and straight, like common iron things,
> But marvelously adroop between two trees,
> Trembling at slightest touch of foot, it swings,
> A span of sudden gloom and cool and a creek's vagaries.

The boy (I know him well) has crept up there
Through the smooth willow's crotch and footed the wire,
Tiptoe where ancient planks have rotted through
And gone, like his wild yesterday's desire,
Into the stream as things that fall asleep where they wanted to.

In the close leaves the rustle tells him to dream.
He knows the sunny rock and the leaping in;
How the pool will jostle its lustres into flight
To and fro,—how minnows touch the skin,
And he hears afar the splash and laughter of others' delight.

But the bridge stirs under his feet, the wizard bridge.
It sways, moving his heart with taunt unrest,
As the close leaves flutter and fall upon the stream,
He thinks of the hill, dark, unclimbed of crest
And must be going there to see the blue mountain of his dream.

Unlike "The Man Who Would Not Die" and "The Swinging Bridge," "Legend in Bronze" has many characteristics of the earlier verse. An unveiled allegory written in Spenserian stanza, it reveals not only Davidson's continued experimentation with forms but his getting closer to his theme. Although his reaction against materialism has not yet led him to search for a rightful heritage, his protest has become more definite: it is aimed at a specific enemy. A symbolic account of beauty raped by mechanism but completely unaware of what has happened to her, the poem in one respect at least looks toward such later works as "Fire on Belmont Street" in which the citizens are oblivious to the spiritual destruction going on all around them.

The period from 1920 to 1925 was most important in Davidson's artistic development. His intimate associations with members of the Fugitive group not only established close and lasting friendships, particularly with Tate and Ransom, but also assisted him in arriving at his theory of the purpose and function of poetry. The intense, analytical criticism which consumed the major portion of the group meetings, the informal discussions between meetings, and the detailed comments made by Tate and others in the margins of manuscripts passed back and forth among the members of the group were of inestimable value to Davidson as he attempted to perfect his art. The assurance that his best efforts, experimental though they were, would be published in *The Fugitive* and, through the pages of that distinguished little magazine, would find an audience among the most interested and sensitive readers of poetry in America must have encouraged him to make the serious study and writing of poetry "the conclusion of the whole matter of living, learning, and being."

That these years were a rather prolonged period of apprenticeship— one in which he was struggling to find the form best suited to his talent and the subject matter (the myth) which would use that form—is suggested by the fact that Davidson chose only seventeen poems from his Fugitive days for inclusion in his *Poems 1922-1961*. Only three or four poems written before 1925 contain the theme characteristic of the later poetry: the search of the modern for his rightful heritage. And even fewer of the verses are written in Davidson's mature manner: the smooth, direct, dignified line composed of simple, concrete, and evocative language, with a tone, though serious and sincere, that often carries ironic overtones.

The period of experimentation ended, however, as his personal convictions, his historical bias, and his intellectual views combined to persuade him that the South was more than an accidental locale for his artistic creations. As he became convinced that the section "still possessed remnants, maybe more than remnants, of a traditional society," his struggle to "unite the form" of his poetry "with the myth that ought to belong to it" was almost won; his search for subject was over. In the period immediately following, Davidson's poetic skill was challenged and his creative energy was consumed by the writing of his most ambitious poem—*The Tall Men.*

CHAPTER 3

"The Long Street"

I The Book of the Fugitives

BETWEEN DECEMBER, 1925, when the last number of *The Fugitive* was issued, and November, 1930, when *I'll Take My Stand* appeared, the interests of the Fugitive group underwent an obvious and somewhat drastic change. No longer content merely to serve the muse, some members of the group became interested in "the price of cotton, the value of real estate, the industrialization of the South, the state of religion. . . [and] the state of science"[1] —matters of little concern a few years earlier—and their creative energies turned gradually from poetry to social criticism. For Davidson the shift was neither sudden nor abrupt. He gradually became aware of the causes of some of the unpleasant aspects of the materialistic modern world—his dissatisfaction with the harsh realities of an unsympathetic society is obvious in his earliest poetry—and, after an excruciating period of self-study, he was able to identify the enemy and to suggest means by which it could be controlled if not overcome. Before he turned to social criticism—and he never turned completely in that direction—he had written his first mature poetry, *The Tall Men;* and his most widely acclaimed poem, "Lee in the Mountains," was written during the period when he was most active as a political and social critic.

After the last issue of *The Fugitive* was mailed in December, 1925, the Fugitives no longer felt it necessary to hold their regular meetings. The "Fugitive experiment" as an organized undertaking was over, and Davidson turned to new tasks. For some time the group had discussed the possibility of publishing a selection of the best poems that had appeared in *The Fugitive* and this project gave a tangible reason, if one were needed, to continue those pleasant, stimulating meetings in the Frank home on Whitland Avenue.

Business responsibilities of several of the most active members would not allow them to devote the necessary time and energy to the magazine. Tate was in New York trying to establish the connections and the reputation necessary to permit him to earn a living with his pen. Warren was fully engaged in graduate school, and Ransom was approaching the period when his primary interest would shift from poetry to philosophic and esthetic inquiry. Davidson's creative impulse turned away from the kind of brief lyric which *The Fugitive* could print, and he begun to plan a series of poems which he called "The Long Street," eventually published as *The Tall Men.*

In the last issue of the magazine, Ransom explained the reason for its discontinuance: "The action is taken because there is no available Editor to take over the administrative duties incidental to the publication of a periodical of even such limited scope as *The Fugitive.* The Fugitives are busy people, for the most part enslaved to Mammon, their time used up in vulgar bread-and-butter occupations. Not one of them is in a position to offer himself on the altar of sacrifice."[2] But, he pointed out, the journal did not cease publication for the reason most little magazines fail. It had enough financial support to continue publication indefinitely; in fact, the magazine's economic condition was the best it had ever been. Nor had the editors lost their interest in poetry; quite the contrary was true. There was plenty of verse available for many issues of the magazine, and the meetings to discuss poetry and philosophy—meetings which had been going on for years before the idea of a magazine was conceived—would continue.

Ransom closed his editorial with the promise that there would be future publications of the group, an idea much discussed in meetings during 1926 and later. In 1925, Davidson had begun a project to get the best of the Fugitive verse between hard covers. For awhile he had considered the possibility of establishing a Fugitive press and had made some effort to raise the money, but he quickly realized that such a project was too ambitious. Apparently as early as 1923, Davidson and others had considered issuing a yearbook. In 1925 he had outlined to Tate a plan for such a publication, but Tate had countered with a suggestion for an anthology—a better choice, he said, because in it the poets could give the "best of the past and a sample of the present."

Davidson immediately wrote a letter to Houghton Mifflin. Since Ferris Greenslet, the representative with whom he corresponded, seemed interested, Davidson began the time-consuming task of collecting poems from other members. For a time, the group discussed the possibility of having an introduction written by an outsider. Among the several names suggested for this assignment were those of John McClure, the editor of the *Double Dealer* who had written so favorably of *An Outland Piper;* Edmund Wilson; and Mark Van Doren. After some discussion it was determined that Tate should ask Van Doren, but the idea was abandoned in favor of Davidson's writing a brief preface when it was learned that Van Doren would expect a fee. Even after this considerable though surely necessary work had been done, Houghton Mifflin decided not to publish the book because, as Greenslet wrote Davidson, so much of the proposed material had already appeared in print.

But the group, most of whom had been disappointed by publishers before, immediately began to seek other means of publication. The project is mentioned in many of the letters exchanged between Davidson and Tate during 1925 and 1926. "In my role of impassioned idealist," Davidson wrote, "I still believe any thing is possible for determined men, and so I believe that a large scale revival or new turn of Fugitive activity is possible."[3] After the manuscript was refused by Horace Liveright and Harper, Tate was more cautious and pessimistic. On March 1, 1927, he wrote: "I hope to give you some edifying and constructive advice about the Fugitive manuscript before long. My conscience gets uneasy, if only because I am at a loss to know how to dispose of it in any likely quarter myself. It lies around here, a constant reminder of the futility of art." After more than a year of submissions and rejections, they were no nearer publication than when they began. A special meeting was called to decide what steps to take. On March 4, 1927, Davidson wrote Tate a detailed account of this meeting: "We had a meeting Monday night. Opinion is like this on the Fugitive *ms*. If you know any likely publishers, it is suggested that you try one or two more. If we are still rejected, we have two alternatives to fall back on: (1) we can raise some funds for guaranteeing cost of publication, perhaps resorting again to our 'patrons'; (2) we can 'salvage' the whole project (in the army sense) and get up a volume of totally new or almost new material. The last is probably the best scheme of all, for we have already been much too slow in getting up our 'anthology,' and if we have a book composed of new stuff we can attract a publisher much more easily." Davidson closed with the suggestion that Tate try Macmillan, Viking, and Harcourt; but Tate's reply, written apparently on the very day he received Davidson's letter, was even more pessimistic than before. Although he promised to try the suggested publishers "in the order named," he had grave fears that "nothing can be done unless we get somebody behind it."

On May 5, nearly two months later, Tate wrote, "the *ms* of the Fugitive is now at Harcourt. I'll have the news in a few days." Eight days later he wrote, "There is no word yet from Harcourt," but on May 26 he announced jubilantly that the volume was accepted. Davidson announced the good news to the "brethren," as he wrote on May 29, and a meeting of all members was called to give Tate the "instructions" he had requested. Davidson reported that, as he had anticipated, "there was little in the way of instructions to be made to you"; the group expressed its appreciation to Tate, accepted the terms of the contract, and gave Tate "full authority to act" for it. Davidson closed by saying that the group was delighted, the "jubilation has naturally some immodest restraint in it, for we have grown to be so cocky that we take an acceptance like this as a perfectly natural thing." He knew that Tate would not misunderstand this last statement, for neither had forgotten that the manuscript had been making the rounds among the publishers for more than a year.

The volume was released on January 8, 1928, as *Fugitives: An Anthology of Verse;* Davidson was represented by nine poems, only one of which ("Fire on Belmont Street") came from the poetry he had written within the past two years. That he was no longer satisfied with the kind of poetry he "had practiced within the closed circles of the Fugitive group" is clear from the letter he wrote Tate as soon as the anthology arrived in Nashville. Although Davidson was well pleased with the printing arrangements and he could not remember any book "Harcourt . . . has put out that is better looking," his feelings about its contents, particularly his own contributions, were mixed:

My impression of the poems is still about as it was. I get more real satisfaction out of reading Fugitive poetry than most that is published nowadays. And I want to say I get the profoundest impression from my re-reading of your "Ode to the Confederate Dead." I am convinced that it stands at the very top of your work. My previous strictures on it were decidedly overdone and may, I suspect, have proceeded partly from my unconscious wrath following your denunciatory remarks on my own book.

As for my own offerings, I am disgusted with them. They don't jibe at all, the Belmont Street thing warring against all the rest. Perhaps they are more indicative than I realize of my own confusion.[4]

II The Tennessee Faust

Davidson's feeling that his poems in the Fugitive anthology "don't jibe at all" stemmed from the fact that the poetry he had been writing for the past two years was vastly different from the experimental verse he had published in *The Fugitive.* Tate's "denunciatory remarks" were made in the lengthy correspondence the two poets had exchanged as each asked for the other's comments on his latest effort.[5] On March 29, 1926, Davidson had expressed his thanks to Tate for commenting on his poetry. "Especially cheering," he wrote, "was your confirmation of my feeling that 'The Long Street' was the best of the lot."

Of the nine sections of *The Tall Men,* which Davidson was still calling "The Long Street" when he wrote this letter, he apparently had completed two: "The Long Street," which appears as the prologue, and "Fire on Belmont Street," the epilogue. However, later comments in the same letter reveal that the plan for the entire poem was already in his mind: "I will perhaps add to it ["The Long Street"], not in the sense of prolonging it; but it is one of a closely related group or scheme of poems which I am gradually building up. These will, in a roughly unified way, present what I intend to be a fairly complex portrait of a person (say myself) definitely located in Tennessee, sensitive to what is going on as well as what has gone on for hundreds of years."

By May 14 Tate had read enough of the poem to form some rather definite convictions about it. "The Tennessee Faust," he wrote, "looks very impressive, and I think you can make it work." But he could not "predict the possible success" of such a poem in "the grand style" because he agreed with Eliot that "there are no more important themes for modern poets. Hence we all write lyrics. We must be subjective." His basic objection, he continued, is that he cannot accept the theme of the poem:

> I think there is one fundamental law of poetry: You cannot create a theme. Themes are or are not available. You can't put your epic of Tennessee into the minds of Tennesseans; the pre-condition of your writing is that it must . . . be already there.
> . . . *The Waste Land* has held people against their will because it exhibits the present state of European culture and tells us what we hate to believe—that our traditional forms are dead.

Of the two pieces included in Davidson's last letter, Tate wrote, "The Tall Men" was by far the better; "The Sod of Battlefields" was too "unorganized"; the sudden shifts of time (in both poems, but "more so in the Sod") were rather "jerkily done"; and the symbolism was too obvious and expected. Although there were many good lines in the poem ("so many I couldn't record my pleasure in them here"), he warned that fine lines will not produce a poem of the order "you are attempting." In addition to the fact that Davidson seemed to be deliberately "muting the fine lyrical quality of the earlier poems," and although "the subject of your proposed epic is appealing," this poem, he wrote, has two major flaws: thinness of effect and incoherence. "The first, I suspect, is due to the fact that you are attempting to envisage an experience of the first order with a symbolism of a lower order. You are trying to write a history of your mind but your mind is not as simple as you think . . . and the result is thinness; the symbols seem trivial." The triviality of the symbols, he continued, brings up the second point—incoherence—because they "will not bear all the emotion you bring to bear" on them and the "disparity produces a jagged, incoherent note." Tate closed in a more encouraging tone: "I hope you write this poem. . . . When a man is a poet, as you are if any man is, poems fail for one reason: the theme is unsuitable. Why not test your capacity for this theme? If you fail, it will not mean that you have failed in *poetry*."

As Davidson later admitted, he felt "some unconscious wrath" because of this denunciation of what he knew to be the first poem to demand all of his creative talent (and perhaps the first of his poems in which "form" and "myth" were unified). His reply to Tate, as always, was calm and appreciative: "I am much heartened that you concede, even with reservations," he wrote on July 14, 1926, "that my attempt is worthwhile." Although he admitted the validity of much of Tate's unfavorable criticism—even the point that "themes are or are not available"—he insisted that his friend's remarks carried implications of errors of which he is not guilty: "I am not writing an epic (Good Lord, surely not an Epic for Tennesseans). I will merely use your phrase and say I'm writing a history of a mind—my mind, to an extent—and therefore I come within your requirements for subjectivity for modern poetry. I conceive of the series of poems as essentially objective, however much I dramatize incidents or people here and there."

On December 27, 1926, Davidson sent Tate a complete manuscript of *The Tall Men* in the same mail by which a copy went to Houghton Mifflin. In the accompanying letter, he asked that Tate read the poem through "consecutively from beginning to end to see how the thing strikes you as a whole." Whether the book was any good or not ("and I flatter myself that some of it is the best stuff I have ever written"), he was glad it was finished so that he could "go on to something else." Then on January 21, 1927, when he had received word that Houghton Mifflin had accepted the poem, he added a final comment: "It would be wrong, no doubt, for you to write The Long Street, but it isn't for *me* to do so."

III The Tall Men

Despite the objections of Allen Tate, *The Tall Men* (1927) clarifies Davidson's development as a poet; for, as Louise Cowan has pointed out, he has never been able "to consider himself as a detached observer of society, isolated from it, and in a sense alien to it."[6] *The Tall Men* is an attempt of the poet to integrate himself with his own personal past and with that of his region. In a letter to his publisher, written when the poem was to be reissued in 1949, Davidson commented on the sources of the background material in the poem. "It is a blend," he wrote, "of what I learned from my folks, ... what I learned from history, and what I myself experienced."[7] His intention was not to write an autobiographical poem; instead, he proposed "to draw a portrait in what the relativists would now call 'time-space' ... of a 'western' American of 'Southern' antecedents and affiliations who had been obliged by the crisis of modern times to examine both his traditional heritage and his future prospects."[8]

Although the poem may not be intentionally autobiographical, the *persona* from whose point of view the materials of the poem are presented has a background very much like Davidson's. His identity is clearly established in the Prologue "The Long Street": he is a modern Southerner examining his traditional heritage in an attempt to discover if he can continue to function as an integrated personality in a society that seems intent upon destroying the eternal verities upon which man has traditionally based his life. The metaphor of the Long Street is more than the old vague trope of life as a journey. Occurring many times in the nine sections of *The Tall Men*, and in much of Davidson's other poetry, the street isolates and identifies the most destructive characteristics of modern life.[9] The figure suggests that the predicament of modern man has been caused by an enemy more definite and deadly than chance or circumstance. The endless, smoke-infested street, where only the steel thews of houses flourish, is so desolate and so sterile that the poet wonders "If anything in this vague inconceivable world/ Can end, lie still, be set apart, be named."[10]

Unwilling to submit to the anonymity of modern life, the *persona* indicates at the beginning of the poem that he is seeking self-identity. He recounts the past in an attempt to find the "permanent and vital stream behind history and behind all the cultural elements going into the making of modern man."[11]

> Yet I would name and set apart from time
> One sudden face, built from a clay and spittle
> Ancient as time, stubborn as these square cliffs
> Of brick and steel that here enclose my steps.

His search for identity is not easy, but he continues to pace the Long Street "where is no summer" and where even spring, the season traditionally associated with new life and new hope, brings only its "blunt friend Death." As a man he is differentiated from nature because "The grass cannot remember; trees cannot/ Remember what once was here." And even natural beauty is not part of his life on the Long Street:

> Where is the grass?
> Only the blind stone roots of the dull street
> And the steel thews of houses flourish here,
> And the baked curve of asphalt, smooth, trodden,
> Covers dead earth that once was quick with grass.

In contrast to the life and vigor of the earth is the curved asphalt on which

> Steel answers steel. Dust whirls.
> Skulls hurry past with the pale flesh yet clinging
> And a little hair. Fevered bones under clean
> Linen. Aimless knuckles of bones
> Within buttoned gloves waving to eyeless sockets:
> "Good day, old friend! Good day, my girl! Good-bye!
> So long, old man!"

The street that modern man must pace is not one of natural beauty; it contains all of the artificial ugliness of his industrial age and is also almost devoid of meaningful personal relationships. But he makes the agonizing journey to see if he can understand himself and his people; it is the only way he can fulfill his obligation to himself and his responsibility to the "dead men under a pall, nameless and choked."

Travels along this street take the narrator first into the past, to the time of the pioneers who had settled the section of Tennessee from which he comes.[12] Davidson wrote that the nine sections of *The Tall Men* were intended "to be a dramatic visualization of a modern Southerner, trapped in a distasteful urban environment, subjecting the phenomena of the disordered present to a comparison with the heroic past."[13] This statement presents succinctly the organizational pattern of the poem. Beginning with the settlement of middle Tennessee by the early pioneers, the poem is concerned with various aspects of the heritage of "a western American of Southern antecedents": the development of ante-bellum Southern society, the Civil War and its disastrous aftermath, the Southerner's participation in World War I, his marriage to a young lady from outside the South, and his attempts to form an integrated pattern of the fragmentary chaos of the 1920's.

The Epilogue, "Fire on Belmont Street," a penetrating analysis of the contemporary scene, creates with almost tragic intensity the crisis of modern times. The aimless, almost purposeless, existence of the "worthy citizen" of the twentieth century, a devout Rotarian or Kiwanian who is distraught over the prospect of his home being on fire, stands in dramatic contrast to the dedicated and purposeful careers of the hunters, the tall men, "whose words were like bullets" and who, tired of "the easy warmth of houses," pushed across the mountains to settle the region of the Cumberland.

Davidson's blank verse is forceful and direct as he recounts, in "The Tall Men," the heroic exploits of the pioneers:

> It was a hunter's tale that rolled like wind
> Across the mountains once, and the tall men came
> Whose words were bullets. They, by the Tennessee waters,
> Talked with their rifles bluntly and sang to the hills
> With a whet of axes.

By twos and threes these tall men appeared in the valleys and on the hills of Tennessee because they had been made restless by the "too-many-peopled world" of Virginia. With them came their "teeming wives" to "rock the hickory cradles" and to mould the bullets for their husbands. And from these pioneers came the first permanent settlers, tall men "who fight/ With a lazy smile, speaking from long rifles."

The first of the tall men was McCrory, who, while standing guard against an Indian attack, thought of how "a girl's neck looked against the gray/ Homespun at candle-lighting time." As he attempted to fill the endless hours of his lonesome assignment with thoughts of Phoebe who lay sleeping in the house below his perch, he wondered why Buchanan had kept fifteen men from the harvest to look for Indians who most likely would never come.

But McCrory's thoughts were interrupted:

> A spatter of hoofbeats in the bottom-grass
> Broke upward to the fort. McCrory jerked
> Awake like a cat and saw a straggling herd
> Of darting cattle, wild and snorting, crash
> Through the plum-thickets and blackberry bushes. What

> Had startled them? Maybe a prowling bear
> Or a nosy wildcat? Maybe something else,
> A nosy Cherokee or Creek? His rifle
> Slid on the steady logs. McCrory peered.

His carefully trained senses warned him just in time, for there they were, "the painted devils, slinking/ Across a patch of sedge. His rifle split/ September midnight dead in two." Unacata dropped with his neck bubbling with blood, Tatoleskee tripped like a steer "beneath the axe," and Kiachatalle fell as he attempted to apply a lighted torch to the roof of the settler's cabin. The battle raged through the night until, as dawn broke, reinforcements arrived from Nashboro. "But now,/ Softly as night, the Red Men all had gone."

Besides McCrory, who is largely imaginary and who foreshadows the experiences of the McCrory who appears later in the "The Faring" section, Davidson wrote of several historical figures, Tall Men whose bravery and courage epitomize the way man once lived among these hills. John Sevier, with the "sword of the Lord and of Gideon" in his hands, "smote the Indian villages/ To dust and ashes" until he "lived in peace."Andrew Jackson exemplified a code that is largely missing from the contemporary scene:

> What makes men live but honor? I have felt
> The bullet biting next to my heart and yet
> I kept my life for honor's sake and killed
> My enemy . . . .
>
> What was it then but honor
> That blazed too hot for British regulars
> At New Orleans? Then all the people knew
> That I was of their breed and trusted me.
> Cowards and lies and little men will pass,
> But honor, by the Eternal, will endure.

David Crockett, the last of the Tall Men, represents all the attributes associated with the earlier residents of his native region—bravery and courage, the insatiable desire for adventure, dedication to a life of principle, and zest for living:

> The corn-shuckings and square dances, the fiddles,
> The barrels of gin and whiskey, the jerked venison,
> Juicy bear meat, hot corn-pone, molasses,
> And the girls giggling in corners—those are the things
> That make life merry. But there came a time
> When I neglected them all, and we made merry

(My Betsey and I) at a different kind of party,
Playing with powder and ball at the Alamo.

But this journey down the Long Street into the distant past—into the exploration and settlement of a region, the beginnings of a civilization—reminds the modern Southerner of the vast differences between the way of life of these Tall Men and his own. He lives when there are no lands across the mountains to explore, no Indians to fight, and few opportunities to demonstrate valor or courage. He has not seen a "friend plunge, furred with arrows, across his plough" or heard "the scream of a woman snatched from the hearth / By painted warriors." Neither has he sung the old songs nor danced the old tunes that made life merry for Davy Crockett. Instead, his experiences have been vicarious and thus less rewarding and satisfying:

I have read a book.
I have loitered by graves. I have trod old floors,
Tiptoed through musty rooms and glanced at letters
Spread under glass and signed *Yr Obt Servant*,
And wistfully conned old platitudes in stone.

His way of life has left the ways of his father. At the end of a day consumed almost entirely in meaningless, futile activity, this "veteran of storm and traffic" folds his paper neatly in his pocket and joins the other "tall men" of his generation for the ride home from the office:

This is dusk
Where tall men humped on cushioned seats glide home
Impatiently. Feet in immaculate leather,
Silken-cased, urge down the throttle gently,
Speeding with effort only of ankle and wrist.

In this world "words pass for bullets." In the morning his "soft proud body" is borne into a "city hoarse/ With nine o'clock which brings the swivel-chair/ And to the hungry brain the pelt of typewriters." He realized that the sweep of something ("call it civilization") across the mountains has left him "like numb and helpless driftwood."

But this modern Southerner, despite the debilitating influences of twentieth-century life, is unlike his counterpart in other sections of the country. When he is asked by the little man with a "Northern way/ Of clipping his words" if the Tennessean is made tall because of the buttermilk and cornbread or because of the air and the many hills he has to climb, the Southerner can reply: "Tallness is not in what you eat or drink/ But in the seed of man." And the blood that runs in his veins is that of the "tall men who walked here when there were/ No easy roads for walking or for riding." For Him at least, the "bright honor," "the ways of fighters," and the songs of his race are not "something read in a book only" or engraved "only in stone." Instead, the memories of these men and women who were his ancestors—their deeds and exploits, their purposeful and productive life—are carried forever in his heart. Thus the *persona* is able from this probing of his past to achieve a part of the purpose stated in the prologue to this series of poems—to "set apart from time/ One sudden face" and see "If anything in this vague inconceivable world/ Can end, lie still, be set apart, be named."

The Long Street, the route that the modern Southerner takes in search of his identity, leads him from the time of the pioneers and the first settlers, the original tall men of his region, to another period of his past, that immediately preceding the Civil War. The tone of the opening section of "The Sod of Battle-Fields" blends perfectly with the closing lines of "The Tall Men." As "The Tall Men" concludes, men of the twentieth century are presented as they "glide home/ Impatiently," "speeding with effort only of ankle and wrist." In the opening lines of "The Sod of Battlefields" one of these men is observed during a leisurely Sunday afternoon drive showing some of the "interesting sights" of his city to an unidentified visitor. Some of the "old ghosts" that are "blown to outer darkness where / The bones of tall men lie in the Tennessee earth" are pleading for recognition as the twentieth-century Southerner of the previous section obliviously goes home to supper. But this modern Southerner does not heed their plea:

Yes, this is the Battery Lane.
So they say. The battle of Nashville was fought
Somewhere around here. I suppose there's a tablet.
We won't go back to look. The Soldiers' Home? . . .
Off yonder through the trees . . . The new paint factory . . .
A little further on . . . . We'll soon be home.

In this century, we are reminded, the Southerner is forbidden to remember his sectional heritage; for "The Union is saved. Lee has surrendered forever." Lee is merely a face, "a granite face on a mountain," "And the grandsons of Confederate soldiers learn about Abe Lincoln, the sad-eyed rail-splitter. Banks close on his birthday." If one wishes to pay "proper respect" to the old men who are symbols of "departed glory," he may participate in the innocuous celebrations of their almost forgotten deeds. But one must remember who was victorious and why, for "The Sod of old battle-fields is washed/ Clean of blood":

> The historic farmhouse where five generals lay
> In bloody dignity is pointed out
> To strangers. Hood is a one-legged fable
> Argued in dusty volumes; Forrest, a name
> Remembered by a few old men in gray
> Stumbling in the hot sun while the hired band plays
> Dixie, and sponsors simper.

One must not concern himself with the past; it is over and would best be forgotten. He cannot mourn for lost battles and for the virtues, either real or imaginary, of a civilization that has passed forever. If the Old South of moonshine and magnolias ever really existed, and there is real doubt that it did, it surely cannot be resurrected; consequently, one must concentrate on the problems of the present. And, if these practical problems become too burdensome, one should leave them to the professionals, persons paid to deal with that sort of thing. As a loyal American, one

> Propounds the pig's conception of the state,—
> The constitution of, by, for the pig,—
> Meanwhile pushing his trotters well in the trough.
> One goes to the movies, motors on Sunday swiftly
> On the baked asphalt.

To the casual visitors, Battery Lane is but a "glimpse of naked trees and a sere/ Whirl of meadows, flashed on the speeding eyes." But, to a few old men "who creep to the sun/ In the winter of a time that heeds them not," it is much more: a "pageant of old wounds and gallantries," "the proof of ancient differences/ Not yet committed to the grave." These ancient few continue to warm their bones with the names of great men long since gone. These men are not merely names to them but "panoplied moments, exultations made/ Visible in the flesh." For them, their memories have specific and concrete reality. Battery Lane is not merely "the symbol of departed glory"; it is the place of bloody, bitter defeat, the place where there was real shooting, not just a background in a movie or a Brady photograph:

> This one has followed Lee. He has clutched the mane
> Of the gray charger and wept farewell. He knows
> Lee was the grandest face that ever looked
> Victory to the conquered. This one has cheered

For Stonewall Jackson, riding the long, gray lines
At Fredericksburg where ranks were steel. Then came
The lunge through Wilderness woods, the fatal moon
Of Chancellorsville, the waving plume of Stuart.
Another dropped at Chickamauga, felled
By the Bloody Pond. Another was taken at Vicksburg.
Another galloped from Donelson with Forrest
And never was taken. . . .

                                                              . . . the dust
Of cavalry gone from a Tennessee road forever.

These are the contrasting and conflicting views that impinge upon the consciousness of the *persona,* the modern Southerner. As the streams of the past and present are continually brought together, he attempts to sift out the elements or influences that make him what he is, to get back to and restate deep sources of racial experiences. In emphasizing the heroic and romantic, the poet attempts "to arrive at some basis for an attitude of acceptance which, while resting on the past, would not wholly reject the present—a mood of positiveness rather than the gesture of defeat to be found, say in *The Waste Land.*" [14] Like the old men and unlike the casual visitors to Battery Lane, this modern Southerner cannot forget that it was the place of battle. He cannot escape a sorrow that dwells, "a valor that lingers, / A hope that spoke on lips now still." His memory is filled with tales that he has "heard and will not soon forget." His grandmother has told him of the Yankees' coming, stealing her family's horses, and burning their barn. *(Why, you won't need your old barn now,/ And so we'll burn it.")* Once a Yankee scouting party searched her home, seeking spies and whatever else they could find:

Then out of the back yard hedge a sudden row
Of eight men in blue with Yankee feet
Violating the porch. Eight men with whiskey-breaths
Bashed into the silence across the carpets, poking
Their long bayonets under the beds and the sofa.
One with a stubby beard and woolly eyebrows
Above a fat chin stuck his Yankee bayonet
Right at a little girl in a flannel nightgown,
Laughing in a whiskey guttural.

The grandmother told the modern Southerner, too, about the anxious days of waiting for news while guns throbbed and rumbled during the Battle of Murfreesboro, about the exploits of Jim Ezell, a Confederate scout justly famous in his day for his courage and daring:

And there was a tale of Jim Ezell and the Yankees,
How he licked ten of them—fifty, maybe—
All by himself. Oh, he was a Forrest scout
And a Chapel Hill boy, you know. The Yankees
Heard he was lying wounded and in bed
At old Dad Smiley's farm up by the creek,
So they sneaked up, all ten of them (maybe fifty),
And the first thing he knew he was surrounded.
Then Jim rared out of bed like a young colt,
Kicked up his heels, spit bullets in their faces,
That-a-way, this-a-way, lit in his saddle fighting,
Bang through the fence and splash in the creek,
And up the dirt road with his shirt-tail flapping.

Then one August afternoon, late in the war, after Chickamauga and the fall of Vicksburg, while his grandmother was playing along in the yard, she observed an event so tragic that she never forgot it, and her account of it to her grandson was so vivid and dramatic that he still remembers it:

Then right past her
A troop of Yankee cavalry, some dismounted,
Dragged three men, three boys in country jeans.
One was Len Smiley, grandmother said, the others
She didn't remember. The boys were arguing
Plaintively with the Yankee captain, swearing:
"Why, Captain, we're no spies. You can't mean
You're going to shoot us. We're Confederate soldiers,
Slipped in home for a snack and a change of clothes."
And as they passed the gate Len Smiley said:
"Look here, Captain. I'm no spy. Why, there's
Becky Patton. She knows me. She'll tell you
I'm no spy, nor no bushwhacker either."

But they took the three young boys, lined them up in the middle of the town, and shot them. One tried to run, and they shot him as he was trying to climb a paling fence. The boys lay where they had been shot until the women and old men picked them up after dark, "dressed them decent," and buried them.[15]

So despite the fact that, as the years pass, "the sod of old battle-fields is washed/ Clean of all blood," he has not forgotten. He remembers not only the tales of his grandmother but also what he has learned from history books:[16] the scouts near Ewell's Farm, "the hurried lines/ Of Federal blue along the Franklin Pike," the bloody battle at Franklin, and the courageous stand of the Confederate troops at Nashville.[17] "Have I forgotten," he asks, "the dead young men whose flesh will not reflower/ But in this single bloom which now I pluck?" Because all of these experiences, regardless of the source from which they have come, are real and meaningful to him, he cannot forget. He learns to live with these memories because he knows they are an essential part of him. Pacing the Long Street in search of his identity, attempting to know himself and to understand his present situation, the modern Southerner must realize fully and completely how and to what extent he is related to the history of his own region:

This is my body, woven from dead and living,
Given over again to the quick lustration
Of a new moment. This is my body and spirit,
Broken but never tamed, risen from the bloody sod,
Walking suddenly alive in a new morning.

In order to assess with reasonable certainty his future prospects, he must understand his present situation, and this understanding will come only after he has established a meaningful relationship with his past. For him, "the neglected ghosts" must never plead in vain for recognition.

IV   The Breaking Mould

"The Geography of the Brain" opens with a devastating comment on the plight of modern man. Although the protagonist, the modern Southerner, has learned much from his probings into his past, he still must live in the present. If his struggle for self-identity is to be successful, he must realize that his attitudes, habits, and beliefs—his very character—have been formed to a very large degree by the society in which he lives. And from this point of view his present situation is not promising; in this setting, the "basis for an attitude of acceptance" that would not "wholly reject the present" is most difficult to discover.[18]

Now mostly intellect, modern man no longer wrestles with the dangerous business of conquering the wilderness and the red man, of attempting on the battlefield to preserve a way of life and a civilization; instead, he lives in a world in which he is almost totally dependent, virtually a slave to paraphernalia and contrivances:

The modern brain, guarded not only by bone,
Afferent nerves, withering hair, and skin,
Requires the aid of a mystical apparatus

(Weights, levers, motor, steel rods, black boy)
And pyramiding dollars nicely invested
To float in boredom up to the cool fifth floor
And a tiled room. "Forward," says King Brain,
And atrophied muscles push two legs along
The usual carpet. Eleven strides, no more,
For unimportant legs while more important
Hands convey a briefcase or fumble keys,
Or click the light for impatient eyes.

In this manner does man in the twentieth century return home in the evening; he returns not, as formerly, to an hour of prayer but to a seven o'clock supper; and he is attended by the groan of trucks, the whirl of a dynamo, and the swish/ Of prisoned waters pumped in tubes of lead." He has almost lost his independence; in order to have his creature comforts, he must use the "Backs and hands of brown and yellow men/ In Singapore or Ceylon," the factories of Birmingham and Pittsburgh, the bellowing steers of Kansas that "go in animals" and "come out packages." His demands are responsible for the "harried eyes of men on subway trains/ And pale children staring from tenement windows." As he settles down in the evening seeking some release from the activities of getting and spending, he is assisted by

> . . . a chair (Grand Rapids) by
> Two slippers (from St. Louis) bites cigar
> (Perhaps Havana) strikes a match (Bellefonte)
> Unwrinkles trousers (Massachusetts) leafs
> The *New York Times* (by U. S. Postal Service).

But now in the quietness of his room his brain "summons up/ The map of all its native circumstance,/ And suddenly it is attended, it is alive." As he looks back down the Long Street, he hears the many "voices out of the blood." He remembers the many stories told him by his father: the long days spent in woods sawing and splitting the fire logs of poplar and hickory; the hoe-cake baked in ashes and the brown new sorghum; the parties and the songs, tales, and jokes of his grandfather; the corn-shuckings with their inevitable feasts of turkey, cake, pies, and cider and fiddlers knocking out "Old Dan Tucker." His father told him, too, stories of his great-grandfather, "the finest gentleman/ That ever lived," neat with beard and white mustache, gloves and polished boots, a thoroughbred who raised blooded horses and kept slaves. "But that is all gone now," his father said.

> On account of the War, and I had rather tell you
> About Julius Caesar or Captain John Smith or read
> Out of Plutarch's Lives. Or sing you the good old songs
> My father used to sing of Barbara Allen,
> Old Rosin-My-Beau, or maybe a funny one
> Like Frog Went a-Courtin'.

In the last two sections of "The Geography of the Brain" the poet attempts to pull together the seemingly unrelated images and episodes of the poem, and he underscores one of its principal themes. The protagonist is enchanted by a "moon of ghosts" and by "old tremulous histories." This land, his heritage, is as rich as a magnolia blossom; but one must not breathe too deeply within "the golden heart" of this "lush flower" or it "will blacken."

"The South," Davidson wrote to his publisher in 1927, "has arrived at a crisis. It has always possessed great individuality which under modern influences it runs a great risk of losing. To retain its spiritual entity the South (as other sections, for that matter) must become conscious of and not repudiate whatever is worth saving in its tradition."[19] Now this crisis confronts the protagonist of the poem. How can he identify those elements in his heritage that are traditionally his as Southerner? And, once they have been isolated—the genuine separated from the spurious—how may they be preserved? The second question, merely suggested here, is considered in more detail later in the poem. His brain, the protagonist says, is attended by "motley splendors": the dust of battles, bones "rotting like antique lace," tales of old men, silk gowns "crumbling in attics," hunting shirts, Bibles, ruffled shirts "of gentlemen in forgotten graves." But, he asks, is he "dreadfully attended" or has he merely had bad dreams? Wherever he goes, he is forever accompanied by these connections with his past; all these streams converge in him as all the westward rivers flow into the father of waters. He is some of all of these; he is what he is and different from all others because of the individual contribution of each of these attendants:

> They stay where they are put,
> Steady within the modern brain which draws
> Attendants grim or beautiful together,
> Asking of motley splendor out of the past
> A stubborn unity of courage, only
> A wall against confusions of this night.

By means of this journey down the Long Street in search of his identity the modern Southerner is one step nearer the objective he set for himself: to name and "set apart from time/ One sudden face, built from clay and spittle." His probings into his past have led him to a consideration of his ancestors "who beat back the best and bravest attempts of the Indians to break the grip of the White Man."[20] Next he comes to the realization that an inseparable part of him derives from the bloody sod of Civil War battlefields. Then his search brings him to consider World War I, the new wave of blood and violence that rocked the land of the Tall Men. Still trying to ferret out the elements of and influences on his background, the protagonist must inevitably confront the most horrible catastrophe of his own day; but now he is dealing with a different kind of experience, not with something he learned "from ... [his] folks and other folks by word of mouth" or "from history books" but with something he has actually experienced:

> Not now the rumored faces of a past
> Far distant urge me into being. These
> Are faces out of a past that still is present,
> Though crusted with time, for still in the twenty-fourth year
> Of manhood I go to war.

The protagonist remembers faces of men who "have passed into mine," scenes "most terrible or dear," and "glares of old battle-fields" on "scarred French hills." Now he is not dealing with the "far-off din of a muffled dream" of a man who knows war only from "black letters daubed across a noisy page"; he relives vividly and movingly his own experiences and those of thousands of other young Americans who returned the visit of the ancient Vikings. This time the direction of travel was reversed, going from west to east, returning to their original home "borne in the Angles' ship" eastward for battle:

> They who were Vikings came
> Back to the Norman shores, with the Norman sinew
> Strong for the oldtime faring, with Norman brow
> And the Norman name, fused, molten, changed.
> Saxon and Norman came to the elder land,
> Jesting in casual tongue, having heard of deeds
> Bruited somewhere in France or in Flanders fields.

His reminiscences recreate the entire experience of the war, from the reception of his orders to report for duty through the tedious details of training and the harrowing scenes of combat, to his triumphant return and reception at Charleston, South Carolina.

"Parting is first," the protagonist recalls, "then hope of return, and then perhaps return."

The tall men travel overseas in "The ship's belly . . . huddled with guns," and they land at Liverpool where "Rumpled khaki poured from the belly of ships/ And the tall men strode . . . through dingy streets." As the Americans march along in even columns, the children along the way ask about the emblem of the wildcat on the soldiers' sleeves.[21] Proceeding through Oxford by train, on their way to Liverpool, some of the soldiers read their official welcome from King George V, beginning "Soldiers of the United States."[22] They arrive at Southampton, "the port of Kings," cross the Channel indifferently, "snoring in tousled groups"; and finally reach their destination, the docks of Havre. After a midnight inspection on a Norman hill by a British major, they board the unfamiliar, almost toylike, little train and ride across the French countryside. As the soldiers annoy the sergeant with requests for the French word for "red wine," and "belly-ache," the English for "mademoiselle," or Arkansas for "big drunk fool," the modern Southerner, who at this moment is very much American, is aware that, although this journey is his first outside his native land, he is nevertheless returning to an important part of his heritage:

> Now they are going
> Somewhere in France on roads where Roman eagles
> Slanted to meet the Nervii or where
> Napoleon, flushed with greetings, galloped from Elba
> A hundred years before.

Written out of a deep-seated dissatisfaction with the literary treatments of the war available in the 1920's, the sections of "The Faring" dealing with the combat experiences of McCrory and his fellow soldiers are as good as any poetry Davidson wrote before "Lee in the Mountains."[23] This McCrory episode balances and reaccents the McCrory experiences in "The Tall Men" section. The earlier McCrory whiled away the lonely hours of his watch thinking of Phoebe who slept in the cabin beneath his lookout station. His reverie was abruptly broken by a spatter of hoofbeats announcing the Indian attack. Now, somewhere in France, his namesake—his great-great-grandson, perhaps— stands high in a niche ("Spaded from rock and earth by hands now gone to some French field") and gazes across the brief strip of war-torn earth that separates his trenches from those of the enemy. He sees nothing and hears nothing; his vigil is so monotonous that he almost falls asleep. But he knows how to obey orders, and he strains his ear "for sounds that death knows how to make." For three straight nights rumors of an enemy attack have "pestered the trench," but all remains calm. Scuffing his cold feet on the "frozen shelf," he hears the sentinel in the next station moving restlessly, making too much noise. As McCrory waits, he remembers "how a girl's/ Deep eyes commanded his in a land far off." He is brought back to reality as suddenly and as decisively as the elder McCrory had been:

> Five quick convulsive strokes leaped up with roar
> Of steel; a long crescendo scream hurled down
> Upon the steady trench. They felt the guns'
> Hot lips speak toward them, winced for the crash, and knew
> The merging drumbeat of the deft barrage.

Against his natural inclination to charge out of his trench in search of his enemy, McCrory waits, as he had been instructed to do, until the "gray-green" men are well out of their trenches and in the middle of no-man's-land. He peers from his parapet; and, when the "line of forward wrenching shapes" is in the proper position, his "war-song" leaps from his whistle, and the tall men fire coolly and deliberately. They see the "helmets bob and topple," the "clenched forms stride and fall." Then, as softly as night, the foe leaves the field; but many lie still "where rifles locked them into slumber," and McCrory stares at the "red/ Numbness that was his arm."

In this entire section Davidson's blank verse functions well. The easy-flowing, run-on lines keep the fast-paced action constantly before the reader and create within him the impression of the horrors of modern warfare. Always the vision is limited to the minute—and perhaps inconsequential—sector of the battlefield in which McCrory and his comrades live, fight, and die. No editorial comments and no ironic overtones intrude as in other sections of the poem; there are no suggestions, subtle or otherwise, that modern man is entangled in some rather sorry institutions. The McCrory of World War I is, as was his ancestor in pioneer days, a well-trained, severely disciplined soldier. Although the modern soldier's actions are a little more mechanical than those of his courageous forebear, they are no less brave. Because the poet is content to present the action without comment, he avoids the taint of false sentimentality.

In the fourth part of "The Faring," in which the poet attempts to portray the fighting man's immediate reaction to the Armistice, the tone of bitter irony which pervades the earlier sections of *The Tall Men* reasserts itself. To the men in the trenches, it is not a time for celebration with "paper fluttering in cloud" and people shaking "very clean hands," as it was in "victorious New York." The tall men say, "Thank God, we'll build a fire at last," as they search for cigarettes and wonder if the rolling kitchens will finally reach the front and bring hot food. In the trenches, there are no thoughts of courage and heroism:

> Heroes are muddy creatures, a little pale
> Under two days' beard with gritty mouths that mumble
> Oaths like the Ancient Pistol; or opening cans
> Of messy beef with brittle bayonets;
> Or winding spiral leggins with eyes alert
> For cockleburrs.

The war and its cessation have highly individualized meanings for each of the men, and particularly do the "living and dead have different tongues for war." First the living speak: the colonel is amazed that the green troops reacted like veterans under fire, and he regrets that his division commander allowed him no chance to earn a silver star; the major has second thoughts about the patrol he ordered to certain death, and he knows that "war is hell,/ But cognac softens it around the edges"; the company commander was too busy to be scared, and he detests most his job of writing letters to families of the dead soldiers, telling "what noble fellows they were" ("But how can I say that Corporal Bell's last words/ Were these: *Come on you son-of-a-bitch?*) The captain wants above all a thick, rare steak, french-fried potatoes, and his hometown paper; the first lieutenant wonders why the German gunners should be allowed to live after they had killed most of his patrol, but he finds something in war he likes and speculates on remaining in service; the sergeant knows but will not tell "what killed Lieutenant Clark; it warn't/ No Dutch-man's bullet./ It come from the rear"; the corporal wonders what he, a lover of peace and the son of a Methodist minister, is doing here "Cleaning/ Something that looks like blood from my rifle-barrel/ And singing: 'There is a fountain filled with blood.' "

Than the dead speak: the airman who fell "far-diving over Conflans" and whose death was "pure as flame"; the artilleryman who was officially announced missing in action because his body was never found:

> I heard the great shell rustling, with its point
> Screaming toward me, and knew it bore my name,
> But slammed the breech and sent my last shot home
> Before oblivion took me, and the winds
> Fluttered the cells that were my body once.

But the most significant comments for the modern Southerner searching for his identity are those made by an Unknown Soldier and by Private Smith. The Unknown Soldier hopes that he and his comrades have not fallen in vain: "Out of this earth that covers me, a pall flung by anonymous hands of men, I cry: Not in vain, O States, not in vain the blood!" Private Smith points up the continuity of the tradition comprising the past of the modern Southerner: the Long Street—the one which he is pacing, attempting to determine if "anything in this inconceivable world" can "be still, be set apart, be named"—is unbroken. Although it appears devious and sometimes faint, it can be followed.

In Private Smith's speech one sees the relationship between the two wars—World War I and the Civil War, an association which the protagonist of the poem undoubtedly makes. He concludes that his body and spirit have risen, "broken but never tamed," from the bloody sod of the battlefields of the Civil War. Private Smith's comments on a war fought nearly three-quarters of a century later are in the same vein:

> *Roses are blooming in Picardy,* sang
> My buddy, John McLaurin, the night before
> We went over the top and he was killed. I think
> That roses will bloom on the Hindenburg Line forever
> Out of the breasts of men. Did I read at college
> Something of Whitman's, saying, What is the grass?
> The grass transpires from the white breasts of young men.
> And roses bloom in the vigilant hearts of friends.

"The Faring" closes with the tall men's triumphant returning and their seeing their homeland for the first time after months of homesickness and realizing that, like all other men, they "find their country beautiful afar." But their exaltation is not long-lived; almost immediately they are faced with the necessity of earning a living in a world completely indifferent to them and to their sacrifices on foreign battlefields. When McCrory, still wearing his army overcoat because he spent the last of his service pay for a railroad ticket home, presents himself at an employment agency, he is met with the question: "Well, what are your qualifications?" His response that he had "learned the Impossibles" in the army succeeds only in provoking the pat, impersonal answer, "We'll file your application."[24]

"Conversation in a Bedroom," the next section of the long poem, is concerned with these immediate postwar experiences. As the protagonist tries to reconcile the incongruities of his sterile modern world and his heroic past, he confronts the most difficult emotional experiences of the poem. Plagued by a loss of faith in a God whose ears are "clogged with pontifical wax," he doubts if "blood can wash out blood," and he vows to seek a "different magic." He calls upon the "antique Devil" whose "ears prick artfully up" at his softest whisper and who appears in the form of a Ringmaster proclaiming:

> Though catalogued as a children's bogy,
> A museum fossil, a biblical fogy,
>   I still retain
> Some powers not quite ornamental,
> Instincts cunningly transcendental,
>   And I maintain
> A private service, guaranteed,
> For invalid souls who are in need
>   Of losing themselves.

Before he performs his services, however, the Ringmaster says that modern man, like Faust, must render up his soul. But the modern is more sophisticated than his ancient brother; he has "read much more than black-letter books, and seen/ A thousand Helens whirled in motor cars"; consequently, he must see what the Devil has to offer before he signs the contract. The Devil agrees, therefore, to show a two-reel movie; the first is "Disease of Modern Man." This portrait, presented in rollicking quatrains "rhymed as fancy indicates," can be contrasted at every point with that of the tall men who transformed an Indian-infested wilderness into a new civilization or with the clearly drawn figures of those who met the enemy at Gettysburg or Verdun. So great is the poet's distaste that he can hardly control the irony and his bitterness:

> This is Rupert of the House
> Of Rupert, famed in history,
> Pondering on his income tax,
> Deducting genealogy.
>
> Great-grandfather from a loophole
> Potted Choctaws in the thicket;
> Rupert, menaced by the Reds,
> Scratches the Democratic ticket.
>
> Rupert's mother D.A.R.
> Rupert's father, U.C.V.;
> Rupert, mounting in his car,
> Zooms up to God in Rotary.

> Grandma Rupert had ten children;
> Rupert's father begot five.
> All of Rupert's stocks and bonds
> Are strained to keep one son alive.

This kind of pettiness and insignificance is obvious in many phases of modern life. Democracy is a "fuddled wench"; the church, "aware of nakedness," parades in "posters and a barrel"; editors distribute "syndicated pap" and promote the "national constipation." Although science is pushing back the utmost bars of space, men are shrinking up into specks. "I cannot bear / This pain of insignificance," modern man says, "Is there no cure?"

The Devil's reply is to show the second reel, which, he says, is much better than the first because it has a happy ending. He presents several "means of sweet deliverance," each of which represents some form of escapism. First there is the Traveler whose thesis is that "the rescue of the wise is only in flight." Although he has "feasted on alien glory" until he is himself no longer, he has found his life. Then a Mystic proclaims that the only way to life is to hoard the truth within. Then three Expatriates are presented: the first has left this impossible "country of bigots and warped schoolma'ams" for Paris, where one "may drink, talk, curse, carry a cane,/ Wear spats, grow a moustache, and admire James Joyce"; the next has discovered what was wrong with him after he had visited Oxford, adopted a British accent, and "become a gentlemen"; the third has found satisfaction only in the most esoteric forms of modern art. The three expatriates are followed by a "Bobbed-Hair Bacchante," who seeks release in the pleasures of the flesh, and by an Intellectual, an academic scholar who has lost himself in the specialized study of an earlier time.

At this point the reel stops abruptly for, although there is more, the protagonist will not see it. For him these "negative freedoms" offer neither rest nor peace. He will not sell out to the devil because he knows that somewhere beyond this nightmare world there are "Green hills where moonlight falls on honest grass/ And honest men who sleep or, waking, speak/ The tongue I speak and love." He will not accept the negative attitudes of his age; he can follow none of the avenues of escape offered by the devil because he must live his life within the context of his own experiences.

For him, the hectic, fevered hallucinations of nerves, insomnia, and the tortured imagination—which he knows as intimately as any of his contemporaries do—present no acceptable solution to his dilemma. Pacing the Long Street, the mind of society in his own day, he must continue his search for identity by absorbing completely the concrete particularities of his own past. He cannot be lured into the broad avenues of baked asphalt trodden smooth by the masses of men seeking an easy escape. Although "the lights bloom up uncertainly" for him, he can "set apart from time one sudden face" only by discovering as exactly and as completely as he can the extent to which he is related to the history of his own region. In this relationship perhaps lies his uniqueness, a partial explanation for his being able to escape the alienation, the loss of faith, the life without direction or purpose characteristic of so many of his contemporaries.

The protagonist's search into his inherited background brings him face to face with the conflict between fundamentalism and modernism in religion. In "The Breaking Mould," his investigation of this conflict begins at that point in the seventh century when King Aedwin was persuaded by Paulinus to accept Christianity. The old Norse gods, who could give man little assurance beyond the present moment, were passing out of vogue. While they reigned, man's life was like Bede's flight of a sparrow "from door to door / Of a hall where men sit feasting, and fire is warm." Man came from cold and darkness, was safe for a moment only, and then moved into "dim and outward winter" again. But there came the time when Aedwin in his "great boar-helmet was seized and won / By a lean priest whose eyes were kindling with dreams / Of the blessed Road." From that moment when the great king was "gentled with Latin hymns," "cleansed with holy water," and "crowned with thorns," Odin, Thor, and Asgard had fallen forever because Christianity had come to the British Isles.

From this beginning, there has developed slowly over the centuries a once-solid mold of tradition, a mold that seems to be cracking and breaking. But this modern Southerner still appreciates the daring and courage of the men who faced the gravest dangers in order to pass along to him this most significant part of his heritage: Martin Luther, nailing the ninety-five theses on the door; the shapers of the Protestant Reformation; and the men and women who fled England, fought the Indians, and settled America. "Are these not blessed," the poet asks, who have been "firm in search of God so many a year?"

> With my father's claymore
> I faced the Sassenach Tyrant at Culloden,
> Then homeless fled to western mountains. There
> The hunting-shirts were bowed at Watauga Old Fields,
> And Samuel Doak, before King's Mountain, prayed
> To the ancient God of battles.

The modern Tennessean reflects upon his own search for God. His early youth was spent in a state deeply involved in an evangelical movement, but the evangelist who offers him a lift is but a coat on a stick when compared to the Evangelist of Bunyan's allegory. He cannot heed the call of the "mashed-out music," the "sweating choir," or the semi-literate minister who bleats

> *Brother, are you a Christian? Are you*
> *Washed in the Blood? Oh, Brother, sinful Brother,*
> *Come while the choir sings Number Seventy-nine*
> *And give me your hand. God bless you, Brother.*

Although the protagonist was reared on the emotional fare of the shallow evangelist and is attracted to the rational explanation of the scientist, he cannot find answers to his fundamental questions in the system of either. Men try to contain God, and put Him into a mold in order to protect themselves from the fear of the unknown. But the soul of the sensitive, inquisitive narrator will not be contained in the "dead/ Plaster that other hands have made. It is cramped/ And like a child within the womb it must/ Begone from that which gave it life."

So the poet's hero continues the excruciating but enlightening process of self-analysis. The "sudden face" that he is attempting "to set apart from time" is a blending of three influences: paganism, Methodism, and secularism. Even after a thousand years he has not learned "the voice of the Hebrew God or the Hebrew way." The poet returns to the Anglo-Saxon past and moves through the development of the Christian culture up to the present, an age dominated by scientific reason. He poses and tries to answer a question: "Can these three forces be harmonized, can they be reconciled?" Can modern man, particularly the one about whom this poem is written, retain his faith despite the contrary evidences presented by his scientific and literary studies?

He surveys, first of all, the many artificial and superficial aspects of the modern church: the doctrinal softness, the adoption of the practices of big business, the neon signs that read "Jesus saves." Nevertheless, as Randall Stewart has observed, one gets the impression that the greatest of these influences is Methodism.[25] The modern Southerner remembers the Ten Commandments taught him by his mother; the Bible which he read through, chapter by chapter, at the age of twelve; the hymns of the country choirs that still "haunt" his tongue; and the youthful prayers that in moments of crisis still arise "unbidden" to his lips. These early experiences are irretrievably a part of his very being, but the paganism is mostly something read about in books, the scientism something imposed upon him by the age of science in which he lives. He is not repudiating God but seeking a God "who will not tame the manliness of men." So he repeats his question:

> How can three alien men be reconciled
> In one warm mind that like the sparrow flies
> In a great hall lit for feasts and the laughter of men,
> And would be glad before it goes forever
> Out of the opening door? Oh, give me a scroll
> Written anew, for where I pass are lions
> Walking chainless and devils that will not flee.

As the protagonist continues to pace the Long Street seeking to find some permanent values, some eternal verities, to give focus and purpose to his life, he comes to a consideration of the most intimate and personal of his attachments, his marriage. In previous sections of the poem, the Southerner has sought a connection with sectional heritage; and, as John Crowe Ransom has indicated, he has made the "groves and straggling legends of Tennessee give up their dead and walk and talk for us."[26] He has enlisted in World War I and fought for a contemporary cause, thus carrying on the heroic tradition as well as he is able. Despite the weaknesses of the modern church and the doubts and dubieties of the scientific age in which he lives, he has found that God still operates even in the unlikely modern world. But his greatest assurance of permanency in "this vague, inconceivable world" is the love he feels for the Ohio girl to whom he is married, "a daughter of winds and lakes" with a "supple, reaching mind that leaps and conquers,/ Vital and passionate after knowledge." In "Epithalamion," a convincing love poem written in a stanza form that echoes Spenser, the modern Southerner finds his most positive assurance that all will not wither as it becomes "mingled with the chaff of time."

As the poem opens, the protagonist, awakened by an autumn storm announcing the coming of winter and the death of another year, is reminded again of his mutability. But, as the thunder rolls and the lightning blazons, the warm hands of the lovers fold in the darkness, and "each knows that each is there." Although time will surely hush the echoes "of these our voices in the walls that bound/ Our lover's meetings," although "we cannot always waken thus/ Remembering the days that make us one," the poet vows that for them their love is indestructible, that, "coming once," it has come to them forever.

In the best tradition of the form in which the poet is working, he asserts that nature conspired to bring the two lovers together; she from Ohio and he from Tennessee have united as those two great rivers merge to form one stream. Although they come from different sections of the country, the poet speculates on the possibility of an earlier meeting between two of their ancestors. He recalls a story of a group of Confederate soldiers stopping at noon before an Ohio farmhouse:

> Shade was thick
> And gentle by the gate. And then there came
> A dark-eyed girl with pity in her glance
> Pity and love for a tired boy in gray
> Who took with grateful lips the cup she poured
> Of water, for love's sake, and looked his thanks,
> And plodded on, when the sharp bugle called,
> With a wistful backward smile. And did you then
> Smile, too, across the gulf of war, and know
> That bayonets cannot prison love? Love is
> More proud and strong than armies with their banners.[27]

Or perhaps there was an even earlier meeting in that distant past when "the fair-haired Goths/ Came a-harrying over the path of the whale" and the eyes of a young herald met those of a young girl "warm through the spears." But eyes had spoken in vain, the poet says; for that day there was battle. Or later perhaps, in the days of chivalry, there were meetings "unfilled and partings/ Sealed with pledges under a castle window" as the knight went forth to meet the challenge of battle in a foreign land.

So their love is stable and lasting, the poet concludes, because it shares the tradition of young lovers that stretches back into the most distant reaches of antiquity. Like those ancient lovers, the modern Southerner recalls that he left his loved one when the bugles "played our reveille for France"; but now he is back.

> Fulfillment of old vows
> And broken meetings lies within a touch,
> A look, a word, the silence of our hearts
> Until a single room becomes the world.

Because the spiritual disorder of the world in which they live is characterized by the absence of myth and ritual, their love cannot be celebrated in the public forms that it would once have been. There are no muses left to sing in "sweet and pagan names the day of love," no viol or rebeck to play for "largesse of this morn," no dancers to move with music to the house where they will stay. The sterile age of science and commerce in which they live does not favor such unnecessary and financially unprofitable activities; yet the protagonist realized that in the sincerity and depth of this human emotion, love, he has discovered a commitment to which he can devote his best energies, a pivot around which his life can move: some beauty remains amidst the smoke-infested streets, the dead earth, the whirling dust, and man with his "fevered bones under clean linen." Thus the poem ends with this admonition:

> Let the long street a solemn music speak
> And larger beauties break
> From this wide world that is our marriage room,
> And April grass and every April bloom,
> And Hymen cry and now your joyance make,
> And drink the skies' sweet influence while ye may.

"Fire on Belmont Street," the epilogue to *The Tall Men,* was written before the other sections of the poem. Completed early in 1926, it won first prize for that year in the Southern poetry contest sponsored by the Poetry Society of South Carolina.[28] In the background material Davidson sent to John Hall Wheelock on February 4, 1949, when Charles Scribner's Sons was preparing to publish *Lee in the Mountains and Other Poems,* the poet commented on the time of composition and his intentions in the poem:

The Tall Men really began with the poem "Fire on Belmont Street," which now stands as an epilogue but was written just before I began the main series of poems. Some readers have lately found in certain lines of "Fire on Belmont Street" what they term a prediction of the atom bomb. Of course it would be ridiculous to say that I knew anything whatever, in 1925, about uranium and its possibilities. Nevertheless it was certainly evident to me that modern science was willing to go to any lengths of destructiveness which modern business would subsidize or for which modern liberals could get up slick excuses. I had also seen some combat in World War I, and I saw demonstrated, at Clamecy, France, in 1919, some of the then "new" weapons, and I felt apprehensive of the worst, during the postwar years. Somehow I could not derive much substantial assurance from Mr. T. S. Eliot's complicated sermons in verse. It did not seem to help me, or the people I valued, very much that the Thunder had said "Da" on the banks of the Ganges. What I wanted to know was whether it was saying anything intelligible and helpful on the banks of the Tennessee, Ohio, and Mississippi, which Mr. Eliot had cold-shouldered.

On another occasion Davidson commented on the "vision" he had that sent him off to write a "kind of poetry far different from that which he had composed in the closed circle of the Fugitive group": "I was possessed by the vision of some plump burgher of Nashville—some devout Rotarian or Kiwanian perhaps—clumsily running at the cry of 'Fire,' thinking only of his own house, as yet unaware that every roof was in danger."[29] In that statement lies the germ of the poem. A worthy citizen becomes frantic with fear that his house may be on fire:

> "Where is the fire?" he babbled as he ran.
> "The fire! The fire!" Spat between pursy breaths
> He dropped his question, stuck his gross right hand
> Against his watch-chain, ran, and stared, and sobbed,
> *Out Belmont Street? My God, that's where I live!*

He is so intent upon learning the fate of his house that he is oblivious to the speaker's warning that the whole city is being destroyed. Like the other respectable citizens he is unaware of the moral softness that is dissolving the core of his society, of the spiritual disorder and fragmentary chaos that have devoured the active faith of his ancestors:

> "The fire," I cried, "What fire? No gables burn,
> Nor is that redness some unusual dawn
> Sprawled against moonrise, nor a dragon's breath
> Spurted from some old sewer you forgot,
> Nor ghosts of Red Men that your fathers knew,
> Come back with devil-medicine to bombard
> Your bungalows. Choctaw and Cherokee
> Lie where the spitting Decherd rifles planted
> Under the Tennessee grass, their tired bones.
> The Fire! What fire? Why God has come alive
> To damn you all, or else the smoke and soot
> Have turned back to live coals again for shame
> On this gray city, blinded, soiled, and kicked
> By fat blind fools."

Where in this modern age, the speaker asks, can one find the courage, the heroism, and common devotion demonstrated by Hnaef and his sixty warriors who were willing to die to save their homes? The modern Southerner, still pacing the Long Street "where is no summer/ But only burning summer," has another question to ask that fat burgher and himself:

> But who will stand tonight,
> Holding this other door against the press
> Of brazen muscles? Who can conquer wheels

Gigantically rolled with mass of iron
Against frail human fingers? Who can quench
The white-hot fury of the tameless atoms
Bursting the secret jungle of their cells?
Oh, who can stay or even chain the dull
Gnaw of the fiery smoke, eternally settling
Into the beating heart? There is no fire?
Only, perhaps, the breath of a Southern wind
That I have known too well in many a summer,
Drying the pulse, stopping the weary pulse,
Blowing the faint blood back in the curdled veins
Till there in no way to think of what might be
Better or worse. Yet maybe it were better
Climbing the tallest hill to cry at night:
"Citizens, awake! Fire is upon you, fire
That will not rest, invisible fire that feeds
On your quick brains, your beds, your homes, your steeples,
Fire in your sons' veins and in your daughters',
Fire like a dream of Hell in all your world."

Thus *The Tall Men* concludes with the plea that man must not forget his heritage; it must not be for naught that the tall men fought and died to beat back the Indians who would drive them out of the Tennessee hills. He must remember Hnaef and his sixty warriors "greedy for battle-joy." A careful reading of the poem reveals Davidson's "feeling of intense disgust with the spiritual disorder of modern life—its destruction of human integrity and its lack of purpose." But in one sense the journey down the Long Street, the current mind of his society, has been highly successful. The journey back through his experiences has not been easy; it has been painful because at almost every point there rose the inevitable comparisons between the heroism and common devotion of the previous age and the physical and spiritual softness of his own; it has been frustrating because the vagueness of the modern world prohibits even the simple act of naming objects.

It is quite clear that Davidson's conception of twentieth-century urban life in 1927 is exactly that expressed by Allen Tate a few years later: the "fragmentary chaos" of the present is a dramatic contrast to the "active faith" that characterized the past. But the exploration of Davidson's modern Southerner is not a vague, nostalgic meandering into a far distant past. He has sought and found a living tradition, a heritage of heroism and humanism. The purpose of his excruciating self-analysis was "to name and set apart from time/ One sudden faces"—to discover his own identity and to understand his present situation by discovering how he is related to the history and the history-makers of his own region. Only through this knowledge can he assess with reasonable certainty his future prospects. In the end, he returns from this excursion into the past determined that he will live in the present, that he will not die in vain, as the Indian did, because he could not adapt himself to the demands of a developing civilization.

Although *The Tall Men,* as Davidson has pointed out, is not intentionally autobiographical, it is obviously a very personal poem. In the recapitulation of the past, in the penetrating scrutiny of the present, and in the obvious contrasts between the two, the poet has discovered "that permanent and vital stream behind history and behind all the cultural elements going into the making of modern man."[30] From the beginning of his poetic career, he had felt that his age was not the happiest one for artistic creation, but before 1925 his interest in the matter was largely academic, a vague feeling undoubtedly shared by all young poets whose efforts are not enthusiastically received. By the end of 1927, however, he was no longer the artist detached from his society, isolated from it, and alien to it. For the first time he was conscious not only of his traditional heritage but of the forces that would destroy it.

The artist had found his subject; from this time forward—in essay, poem, debate, and newspaper article—Davidson expressed his disgust with the spiritual disorder and lack of purpose of modern life. He had arrived, with *The Tall Men,* at a basis for an attitude of acceptance, which, while drawing on the past for its pattern, did not wholly reject the present. Davidson said that he was trying to create "a mood of positiveness, rather than the gesture of defeat to be found, say, in The Waste Land."[31] His affirmation is embedded in his conviction that the present struggle must be to retain spiritual values "against the fiery gnawing of industrialism." He is no longer content to be a detached intellectual artist; and his future career can best be understood in terms of his attempt to "retire more deeply within the body of the [Southern] tradition to some point when he can utter himself with the greatest consciousness of his dignity as an artist."[32]

CHAPTER 4

The Fierce Faith Undying

IN HIS excursions into his personal heritage in *The Tall Men,* Davidson had been impressed with the contrast between the heroism and common devotion of his pioneer forebears and the spiritual and moral softness of the citizens of the present era. But he had found a heritage of heroism and humanism, "a mode of positiveness," from which he could combat the moral sterility of his own age. In *The Tall Men* the poet ranged over his entire heritage from the time of the early pioneers who explored and settled his section of the middle South to that of their great-great grandsons, the soft, ineffectual weaklings who glide home from work "humped on cushioned seats" and who babble futilely about the fires that are destroying their homes. In his next volume of verse, *Lee in the Mountains and Other Poems* (1938), Davidson focused his attention upon one period of his past, his Confederate heritage. The Civil War and its aftermath was to Davidson one of the most catastrophic occurrences in America's history, and his reflections upon its disastrous consequences were extremely painful.

I The Confederate Heritage

The individual poems in this volume demonstrate that Davidson regarded the Civil War in much the same way that Faulkner did. *The Unvanquished,* Faulkner's most sustained treatment of the war, depicts the destruction of the Southern social order and delineates the process by which any society may be destroyed. Always confronted by forces bent on its destruction, the social order must hold in abeyance these destructive elements "by rules and orders, accepted habits and the convention of property."[1] The Civil War was the first *total* war in American history, the only one in which all rules were violated. It was not possible to exert the necessary energy to maintain balance and control; consequently, the destructive elements could not be contained, and the disorder and chaos following the war provided the opportunity for Snopesism to dominate Yoknapatawpha County.[2] In the *Lee* poems Davidson is focusing upon the Civil War and Reconstruction, the period of history in which the deterioration of the traditional social order began.

Davidson's interest in the developments of the twentieth century and his reflections on his personal heritage in *The Tall Men* had led to a study of American history, particularly of Civil War history. This interest figured prominently in the many essays he published between 1930 and 1936 in defense of his Agrarian principles. During the early 1930's he was also writing the series of poems which he published as *Lee in the Mountains and Other Poems.* "Soon after the publication of *The Tall Men* in 1927," he wrote John Hall Wheelock, on February 4, 1949, "I set out to compose a series of poems—largely narrative in character—in which I would attempt to present some of the major figures of Southern history, at decisive or tragic moments in their careers." Although the poet does treat some of the Southern heroes at crucial moments of their careers—Lee, Forrest, and Jackson, for example—to the reader of Davidson's early verse it is obvious that the poet is continuing his journey down the Long Street trying to "set apart from time/ One sudden face." He focuses upon the Civil War not only because of its personal significance to him as Southerner but because in the tragic consequences of that disastrous occurrence he finds the destructive elements that have rendered his powerful, resourceful tall men impotent and hollow.

The metaphor of the Long Street, the poet's journey into the past in search of the cultural elements that combine to make modern man, is carried into "Aunt Maria and the Gourds." The *persona,* one who has made the agonizing investigation into his past, speaks to an unidentified listener, apparently a young man of Southern origin, who is not yet fully aware of the dramatic contrast between the "fragmentary chaos" of the present and the "active faith" of the past:

> You who walk in callous innocence,
> Pacing, as once I paced, the long street,
> Pause, look down, remember how this stone
> Slid and avoided when you set your foot.
> Hear the rattle of gourds over Babylon.
> Learn what the years have whispered secretly;
> Learn how the stone refused your heel and may
> Again miss and waiver, and hurl you on
> Stumbling to what awaits beyond the corner.

The speaker would share with his young friend his attempts to discover his own identity through excruciating self-analysis. Now an older man who has learned much from "Pacing the long street where is no summer," he would like to spare the young man some of the discomforts and dangers of this perilous voyage.

Unless the modern Southerner is as insensitive as the hollow men who see nothing but shadows in "this vague inconceivable world," he is certainly aware that drastic changes have come to his beloved land. Aunt Maria, who keeps the old place to die in but who, in the meantime, is "home Thursdays at four o'clock," symbolizes the Old South. The forms of the old civilization remain, but the substance is gone:

> Aunt Maria, to whom all doors are open
> Knocks at none. Who are they, living now
> Behind old doors where once her carriage stopped?
> The Devil looks out for his own. The Devil has taken
> Cherry and Spruce streets into the kingdom of Hell,
> Lopped the trees, put in his plate-glass windows,
> Smartened the ruins with optimism and paint,
> As was foretold in Sixty-five.

More despairing of urban civilization than even "Fire on Belmont Street," this poem fixes the blame for man's present tragic circumstances. The "fiery gnawing of industrialism," the enemy hinted at in *The Tall Men,* is clearly delineated in this poem and in many others in *Lee in the Mountains and Other Poems.* The future prospects of mankind are far from bright; indications of portentous developments are "Written in blood and readable to the wise." Each spring Aunt Maria plants her gourds at the edge of the porch "where the dark shadow of doom / Speaks, when the ominous winds of March are near." Then in November the dry gourds, the only fruits now matured in the once productive South, rasp "An innocent fatality of song." The protagonist, who has explored every area of his region's past, understands the song and attempts to interpret it:

> Leaning at twilight over the window-sill,
> Looking toward Nashville, neglecting the candles and voices,
> I heard the gourds' foretelling, I felt the hollow
> Rattle of voices singing of Babylon:
> Of Babylon, to whom the years have whispered
> Predictions that the builders cannot now
> Confound with any charm or reassurance.
> Vibrations deep, imperative as death,
> Wrench and shiver.

As the speaker and the younger man prepare to leave Aunt Maria's after one of her four o'clock "at home's" on Thursday, "The wind blows and/ Cumberland waters run / To carry us home." There, beneath the bluffs of the river, "Something stirs that once had life":

> It drops
> Into the stream, a last act of faith.
> Seedballs of sycamore, incautious leaves of willow,
> These have outstayed their autumn, teasing death
> Only so far, not yet beyond all patience.
> Now they let go.

But this faint glimmer of hope, the last gasp of a once vigorous civilization, is discernible only in the country. In the city, man's devotion to progress, or to the false promises of industrialism, have obliterated any sense of a continuing, vital tradition. The obsession for acquiring material possessions has made the modern Southerner oblivious to "a manner of living in which grace, leisure, spiritual and aesthetic experiences" are possible. Man is losing respect for the natural world; he no longer regards nature as something mysterious. Falsely believing he controls nature, he considers it as merely a force to be harnessed for his benefit. He is no longer willing to submit "to the general intention of a nature that is fairly inscrutable."[3] "On Cherry Street there are no leaves to stir, / And no faith, even to die."

But Aunt Maria still clings to a life of order; and, as her visitors depart amid the ominous song of the gourds, she pleads: "Do not forget!/ Come back! Remember! Take my love to all!" The poet, whose meaning is clear, is asking the modern Southerner: Are you aware of what you once possessed? Of what you are allowing to disappear? Will you be so thoughtless and shortsighted that you will discard your tradition completely?

In almost every poem in the volume the poet reiterates his scorn for those who would desert a sacred tradition and accept a system that would dehumanize man and submerge him in the frantic struggle for material possessions. In "Randall, My Son" a young man heeds the cries of a cold mistress—the outside world—and forsakes his ancestral home. The speaker, a Southern woman, this time conscious of her traditional heritage and of the forces that would destroy it, asks her son if he realizes the significance of what he has done:

> Within the changeless room where you were born
> I wait the changing day when you must go.
> I am unreconciled to what I know,

> And I am old with questions never done
> That will not let me slumber, Randall, my son.

Because the young man has broken the tradition and heeded "the cries/ That lure beyond familiar fields," he will bequeath to his own son, "not born or yet begotten,/ The luster of a sword that sticks in sheath,/ A house that crumbles and a fence that's rotten." Again the speaker pleads that the young man not chase after false gods. In an obvious reference to the Agrarian movement, the poet suggests an alternative: "Hear, what I hear, in a far chase new begun/ An old horn's husky music, Randall, my son."

In the Introduction and in many of the essays, the authors of *I'll Take My Stand* insist that the arts cannot flourish in an industrial society. The artist's creative insight functions best within fixed and certain social boundaries which allow "a free and disinterested observation of nature that occurs only in leisure." The proper understanding of the work of art and its relationship to the society that produced it is impossible in an industrial regime "except by some local and unlikely suspension of the industrial drive."[4] This premise is illustrated in "On a Replica of the Parthenon," one of the most successful poems in the *Lee* collection. The solemn, declamatory tone of some of the other poems becomes bitingly ironic when the poet considers the rootless culture which ignores its own heritage and erects in Nashville a life-sized model of the Athenian temple. The aimlessness of a society that worships senseless change and impermanent values is disgustingly evident when its leaders "raise up this bribe against their fate." This pretense of a love of tradition is a "dim last / Regret of men who slew their past."

The very attempt to reproduce one of the lasting monuments to man's creative genius is an absurd example of the modern misconception of the function of art that is held by a people who desperately attempt to cling to the form but who have not the remotest conception of a Classical civilization. The "aimless motors," a recurring symbol in Davidson's poetry for the purposeless energy of the modern world, provide a startling contrast to the pristine simplicity of the Grecian civilization out of which the original Parthenon came. "What do they seek," the poet asks, "who build but never read their Greek?" The incongruity of this so-called public cultural act can only make the "incertainty" of the society that committed it "more sure." The construction of the accurate reproduction is the feeble gesture of a people whose artistic sensibilities have atrophied under the dehumanizing demands of an industrial community:

> Shop-girls embrace a plaster thought,
> And eye Poseidon's loins ungirt,
> And never heed the brandished spear
> Or feel the bright-eyed maiden's rage
> Whose gaze the sparrows violate;
> But the sky drips its spectral dirt,
> And gods, like men, to soot revert.

Other poems convey Davidson's "feeling of intense disgust with the spiritual disorder of modern life,—its destruction of human integrity and its lack of purpose."[5] In "The Deserter: A Christmas Eclogue," a Confederate veteran is listed on the rolls as a deserter because he leaves his military company to go home, only two miles away, to warn his family to flee before the Yankees overrun the community. By a pathetic turn of fortune he is captured before he can regain his outfit. At the time, he had no particular difficulty because "In sixty-five men took my word, men knew/ That Jamie Hines was captured near Pulaski/ Trying to reach the army." But now the situation is different: government has become an impersonal organization that prefers the "written word to any word made flesh." Now no man's word is his bond; the written word says Jamie Hines is a traitor and so he will remain.

Jamie's friend Lester who listens to the story, exclaims, "You've lived too far away these years/ And kept your mind too innocent to know/ That word is no more bond." The people who control the world's affairs do not "Trust the ancient charity of their hearts/ Unless incorporated, checked and mapped." This world is run by deceit and guile; and, if one is to succeed, he must adopt its weapons. The mistrust of human motivation in the modern world is an unwholesome contrast to the active faith of the past, and the force responsible for the destruction of the traditional heritage is clearly identified.

> Nashville was occupied by Federal troops
> In eighteen sixty-two. *They hold it still!*
> The only difference is, they do not wear
> Blue uniforms.

This tone of bitterness and vindictiveness dominated many of the poems—for example, "Two Georgia Pastorals"—poems in which the poet becomes so personally involved that his involvement encroaches

upon the point of view he has established for the poems. Few readers of
"The Deserter: A Christmas Eclogue" can receive the lines quoted
above as merely a dramatic utterance. Davidson is more effective when
he is less argumentative, when he does not disrupt the poetic experience
with a bold, direct statement of opinion. The contrast between the
aimlessness and uncertainty of the present and the purposefulness of
the past is handled more convincingly, therefore, in such poems as
"Twilight on Union Street" in which the basic conflict is presented in a
less direct or more suggestive manner. In that poem Davidson sketches
briefly the three stages in Andrew Jackson's relationship to the people
of Tennessee; each stage is given a quatrain, and the time of day in
which the action occurs suggests the period of Jackson's career under
consideration. In the first quatrain, the young Jackson is vigorous,
aggressive, and purposeful:

> In the cool of morning Andrew Jackson came,
> A young man riding on a horse of flame,
> Tossed the reins to a black boy, and strode
> High-booted and quick-oathed to court and code.

In the second, the mature Jackson is grim soldier, respected statesman,
and honored leader—a tall man who follows his own concept of honor
regardless of what others say or think:

> Of a sultry noontime General Jackson stalked,
> A grimness that put silence where men talked.
> The fluttering of the gossips thinned and fled;
> They knew where General Jackson left his dead.

But now comes the twilight: the old era is passing, and men look
elsewhere for leadership. Like the blind crab in Tate's "Ode to the
Confederate Dead," modern man, who has motion but no direction,
dissipates his energy in following blindly the line of traffic, wherever it
leads. In the dusk no one knows his way; no one is aware of Jackson
and of what he could mean to rootless moderns:

> And now the twilight. History grows dim.
> The traffic leads, we no more follow him;
> In bronze he rides, saluting James K. Polk,
> His horse's rump turned to us in the smoke.

Davidson's Agrarian views are everywhere present in these poems. In
"The Tall Men" he had pictured the modern urban community as
purposeless and as almost meaningless—as an existence without life:

Only the blind stone roots of the dull street
And the steel thews of houses flourish here,
And the baked curve of asphalt, smooth, trodden,
Covers dead earth that once was quick with grass.
Snuffling the ground with acrid breath the motors
Fret the long street. Steel answers steel. Dust whirls.
Skulls hurry past with the pale flesh yet clinging
And a little hair. Fevered bones under clean
Linen. Aimless knuckles of bones
Within buttoned gloves waving to eyeless sockets:
"Good day, old friend! Good day, my girl! Good-bye!
So long, old man!"

In poem after poem in *Lee in the Mountains and Other Poems,* these convictions receive fuller and more forceful poetic expression. Davidson reiterated his impression of an urban wasteland; and in some poems— "Aunt Maria and the Gourds," "The Last Charge," and "Randall, My Son"—he utters a prophecy of doom for the modern industrial society. The emphasis is always on the necessity of preserving one's tradition, but the poems are often so declamatory and argumentative that the poet emerges as the injured prophet—as one who has foreseen and suffered. But in "Sanctuary" he reaches a kind of affirmation which is strengthened in "Lee in the Mountains" and carried forward to such poems as "Lines Written for Allen Tate on His Sixtieth Anniversary" and "Meditations on Literary Fame." Essentially, this reconciliation and acceptance are based on religious resignation.

After the destruction that has resulted from too-rapid change, the poet asks: what does man do now? After the enemy has been isolated and after man has seen the soil given up to asphalt and "square cliffs of brick and steel," should he merely "close the ivory gate with hopeless stare?" Or should he continue to fight? And if so, how? Like the Psalmist of old, the poet says in "Sanctuary," that man should lift up his eyes to the hills, free himself from the entangling encumbrances of an artificial civilization, and seek a sanctuary as his forefathers did.

Man lives in perilous times, an old man warns his young son, and there will be much fighting, for the enemy is intent upon destroying everything man holds sacred. The old man tells the young man to remember and tell his sons, for man must have resourceful and dedicated sons to preserve and continue the tradition:

> . . .if ever defeat is black
> Upon your eyelids, go to the wilderness

> In the dread last of trouble, for your foe
> Tangles there, more than you, and paths are strange
> To him, that are your paths, in the wilderness,
> And were your fathers' paths, and once were mine.

Man has to shed the nonessentials of this ugly and vulgar civilization, the old man urges; he must return to the land where life is peaceful and serene:

> Do not wait until
> You see *his* great dust rising in the valley.
> Then it will be too late.
>
> . . . . .
> Do not look back. You can see your roof afire
> When you reach high ground. Yet do not look.
> Do not turn. Do not look back.
> Go further on. Go high. Go deep.

In the valley every roof is ablaze, the city is on fire and the only way to escape "*His* dust and flame" is to seek the "secret refuge of our race." The contemporary industrial civilization is self-destructive, and the only way to escape the holocaust is to return to nature, to the earth created by God for man. Once there, man should forget destruction, and attempt to reestablish the proper relationship between himself and nature. Man will destroy himself if he continues his amoral quest to change the world, to harness nature, to reduce it to a commodity. For nature that can be so manipulated is no longer nature but an oversimplified picture of it; man must regain a "sense of nature as something mysterious and contingent."[6] If, in the proper attitude, man lifts his eyes to the hills and asks, "From whence does my help come?" the answer will be unmistakably clear: "My help comes from the Lord, who made heaven and earth."[7]

II Victory to the Conquered

"Lee in the Mountains," the title poem of the volume, is Davidson's best-known and most widely anthologized poem.[8] In it, Louise Cowan says, Davidson's "epic dignity and his purity of tone are at their best."[9] Lawrence E. Bowling calls it "one of the very few best poems dealing with persons and events in American history."[10] Soon after the poem was completed on January 15, 1934, Allen Tate wrote Davidson: "Your Lee poem is the finest you have ever written. I say this after much meditation and study of it. I thought your other recent poems, in the last couple of years, too argumentative and documentary. This new one is about Lee and about a great deal more than Lee. It is a very fine poem. If you lose what you've got here and relapse into documentation, I shall come over and cut your ears off!" [11]

Written during the fall and winter of 1933-34, a time when Davidson was formulating some of his most uncompromising defenses of his Agrarian principles, this poem succeeds because the poet is able to unite the form of the verse with the myth that ought to belong to it.[12] In the tragic, final days of one of America's few truly great heroes, Davidson could see a profoundly moving example set by a man whose every act exemplified a life of principle and honor. Here with "the grandest face that ever looked/ Victory to the conquered" was the noblest of the tall men—one whose greatness of soul compelled him to choose what he felt was the right even when another choice might have been of more immediate personal advantage.

The total purpose of the Agrarians, Davidson has said, was "to seek the image of the South which he could cherish with high conviction and to give it, wherever we could, the finality of art in those forms, fictional, poetical, or dramatic, that have the character of myth."[13] Since Lee, for not obvious but plausible and convincing reasons acted in a manner to illustrate the "living tradition, a heritage of heroism and humanism," the poet does not have to strain his material in an attempt to get a sympathetic hearing. He does not have to plead in Lee's defense; properly presented, the case can rest on its own merits. The poem avoids, therefore, the argumentative and documentary tone that Tate finds in much of Davidson's other verse of the period because, for one of the few times in his career, the poet has found his subject; for at least once he could "enjoy and use his rightful heritage and still be in . . .[a] true sense a Southern writer."[14]

The poem covers the period between 1865 and 1870 while Lee was president of Washington College. Its content, presented through Lee's stream of consciousness, may be divided into five parts. In Part I (11. 1-17), as he walked across the campus toward his office, Lee is greeted by a group of students who are seated on the steps of the main college building awaiting the bell announcing the daily chapel which begins each school day. In Part II (11. 18-52), Lee goes into his office to resume the labor that consumed most of his free time during these years, a revision of his father's memoirs. In Part III (11. 53-80), Lee ponders a question to which he must have given much attention in these crucial years: instead of attempting to justify his father's misunderstood career during and after the Revolutionary War, why is Lee not concentrating on his own experiences in the Civil War? In Part

IV (11. 81-103), he gives the reasons for his choice and explores his present situation. In Part V (11.104-121), Lee's reminiscence is interrupted by the bell calling him to chapel; as he prepares to join the waiting students, he contemplates the advice he must give the young men who look to him for inspiration and leadership.[15]

The draft of "Lee in the Mountains" which Davidson sent to Tate on January 15, 1934, opened with these lines:

> Walking into the shadows, walking alone
> Where the sun falls through the ruined boughs of locusts,
> Up to the president's office. Hearing the voices
> Whisper, *Hush it is General Lee!*

Tate commented that this opening was "too pat and abrupt." What was wanted, he continued, was "a more halting introduction to the theme, as if from the scattered images of a moment a line of meditation suddenly took hold and went through to its end."[16] The opening was too "oratorical"; it should be more "dramatic." Tate then proceeded to his most helpful suggestion: "at the end of the passage why not interpolate a line or two or three of perfectly inconsequential observation on Lee's part. Make him see for a second a pile of rocks by the path, or a bush, on the fringe of his growing meditation. . . . Just make him say: I must have those rocks moved; or that spirea will bloom in two weeks; it should be trimmed."[17] Then in a postscript Tate added Caroline Gordon's comment that Lee might address his "casual remarks to some boys standing by."[18]

Tate's comments seem to have stimulated the creative activity that greatly strengthened the first section. When the poem was first published in the *American Review* for May, 1934, its opening section read

> Walking into the shadows, walking alone
> Where the sun falls through the ruined boughts of locusts
> Up to the president's office. . . .
>   Hearing the voices
> Whisper, *Hush, it is General Lee!* And strangely
> Hearing my own voice say, *Good morning, boys.*
> *(Don't get up. You are early. It is long*
> *Before the Bell. You will have long to wait*
> *On these cold steps. . . .)*

As Tate suggested, the interpolated remarks are addressed to the students; but they are not, however, "casual" and "inconsequential" but closely related to the rest of the poem. In fact, they set the tone for the opening section and suggest the conflict of the entire poem. As Lee walks across the campus from his home to his office, he is observed by some students sitting on the steps of a building and waiting for the bell that starts the day's activities. One student calls the attention of the others to Lee's arrival with "Hush, it is General Lee!" They all rise to speak to him. Although Lee has certainly heard the student refer to him as "General"—and this fact will affect his meditations later—he makes a seemingly casual comment: "You are early. It is long/ Before the bell. You will have long to wait/ On these cold steps . . . ." Since the persons to whom Lee is speaking have been identified and his reason for speaking explained, the reader is not disturbed that the poet abandons for the moment Lee's point of view. In fact, as Tate had foreseen, the interpolated remarks do not "violate" the "form"; instead they help to establish it.

But Davidson does not follow Tate's suggestion completely. The apparently casual remarks, the reader immediately realized are both relevant and significant. Not only will the young men sitting on the steps have long to wait before the bell anounces the opening of the daily devotions; they must wait even longer for a new day of happiness and prosperity to come to the South. After the brief interruption, the poet immediately returns to Lee's mind; and the civilian Robert Lee's mediation centers on the remark he has just made:

> The young have time to wait.
> But soldiers' faces under their tossing flags
> Lift no more by any road or field,
> And I am spent with old wars and new sorrow.
> Walking the rocky path, where steps decay
> And the paint cracks and grass eats on the stone.
> It is not General Lee, young men . . .
> It is Robert Lee in a dark civilian suit who walks,
> An outlaw fumbling for the latch, a voice
> Commanding in a dream where no flag flies.

Although the young men waiting on the steps "have time to wait," Lee realizes that he does not because he is "spent with old wars and new sorrows." What he can do, he must do now; and there will be no time to try to rectify the results of an erroneous decision. Lee's dilemma is clear: he has no authority; he is literally an outlaw in his own land. Yet he knows these young students—many of whom were once his soldiers—rely on him for direction. Without violating his own sense of honor how can he encourage these young men to hope for better days in their homeland? How can he assist them in maintaining their integrity and their belief in the enduring virtues of the society that produced them when everything they value seems "maimed, defeated, lost, impugned"? This conflict, dramatically suggested by Lee's comments to the students and developed in the lines immediately following, is resolved in the concluding section of the poem, but not before Robert Lee has done considerable soul-searching.

The diction of this first section also sets the tone for the agonizing self-analysis to which Lee subjects himself. The "old wars" have brought the "new sorrows" which must have plagued Robert Lee every day of the five-year period covered in the poem. The terrain in which he must fight the most important battle of his career is desolate; he must follow the "rocky path" where the "steps decay," the "paint cracks," and "grass eats on the stone." This setting is hardly conducive to the courage and hope he desires to instill in those who look to him for consolation and guidance. In his "dark civilian suit" Lee suggests a mourner lamenting the loss of someone or something valued and loved. His feeling of ineffectiveness is suggested by his reminder that he is "not General Lee"; he is an "outlaw," a "voice/ Commanding in a dream." Surely he is fully aware of the seriousness of his predicament; anything he is able to do, it seems, must certainly fall far short of his young students' expectations. But, although he is deeply troubled, he does not despair. He does not cease to struggle; he is "fumbling for the latch" that will open the door, that will reveal to him the way he should go, the course of action he should take. What he can, should, and must do, and why, is the content of the next three sections of the poem.

The phrase "fumbling for the latch" serves another function, for Lee has come to the door of the building in which his office is located. He enters and prepares to resume the labor that consumed many of his leisure hours during the period of his life covered in the poem: the preparation of a new edition of his father's *Memoirs of the War in the Southern Department of the United States.* Professor Lawrence E. Bowling has demonstrated that a knowledge of Light Horse Harry Lee's career is essential to an understanding of this section of the poem.[19] After an illustrious career as a military leader in the Revolutionary War, Harry Lee made some unsound financial investments. When he could not meet his obligations, his home and other personal possessions were seized by his creditors. Later, while in a debtor's prison for more than two years, he wrote a large portion of his *Memoirs.*

After Harry Lee's release from prison, he opposed America's entry into the War of 1812 and was severly crippled by a pro-war mob in

Baltimore. Much dejected, he left his family in the summer of 1813 to try to recoup his fortunes in the West Indies. After five years he became seriously ill and died before he could return home. During the Civil War, Robert Lee visited the grave and, according to legend, vowed to avenge the wrong done his father. Some speculate that Robert Lee edited his father's *Memoirs* to keep this vow. Davidson uses many of these historical facts and logical suppositions in the second division of the poem:

> My father's house is taken and his hearth
> Left to the candle-drippings where the ashes
> Whirl at a chimney-breath on the cold stone.
> I can hardly remember my father's look, I cannot
> Answer his voice as he calls farewell in the misty
> Mounting where riders gather at gates.
> He was old then—I was a child—his hand
> Held out for mine, some daybreak snatched away,
> And he rode out, a broken man. Now let
> His lone grave keep, surer than cypress roots,
> The vow I made beside him. God too late
> Unseals to certain eyes the drift
> Of time and the hopes of men and a sacred cause.
> The fortune of the Lees goes with the land
> Whose sons will keep it still. My mother
> Told me much. She sat among the candles,
> Fingering the *Memoirs*, now so long unread,
> And as my pen moves on across the page
> Her voice comes back, a murmuring distillation
> Of old Virginia times now faint and gone,
> The hurt of all that was and cannot be.
>
> Why did my father write? I know he saw
> History clutched as a wraith out of blowing mist
> Where tongues are loud, and a glut of little souls
> Laps at the too much blood and the burning house.
> He would have his say, but I shall not have mine.
> What I do is only a son's devoir
> To a lost father. Let him only speak.
> The rest must pass to men who never knew
> (But on a written page) the strike of armies,
> And never heard the long Confederate cry
> Charge through the muzzling smoke or saw the bright
> Eyes of the beardless boys go up to death.
> It is Robert Lee who writes with his father's hand—,
> The rest must go unsaid and the lips be locked.

Apparently Robert Lee is preparing his father's *Memoirs* for the press so that history will have an accurate record for judgment. He was so young when his father left that he hardly remembers him, but his mother told him much of his father, "Fingering the Memoirs, now so long unread." As Lee's "pen moves on across the page," he remembers not only his father but also his mother, whose voice, as he recalls it, is a "murmuring distillation/ Of old Virginia times now faint and gone,/ The hurt of all that was and cannot be." He will complete the *Memoirs* because of a vow he made beside his father's "lone grave": to do so is "only a son's devoir/ To a lost father."

There are other more compelling reasons why he must supply the facts of Harry Lee's career for posterity; and for even more urgent reasons the son cannot comment on his own experiences in the Civil War. The necessity of avoiding a discussion of his own career ("The rest must go unsaid and the lips be locked") is considered in the next section of the poem:

> If all were told, as it cannot be told—
> If all the dread opinion of the heart
> Now could speak, now in the shame and torment
> Lashing the bound and trampled States—
>
> If a word were said, as it cannot be said—
>
> I see clear waters run in Virginia's Valley
> And in the house the weeping of young women
> Rises no more. The waves of grain begin.
> The Shenandoah is golden with new grain.
> The Blue Ridge, crowned with a haze of light,
> Thunders no more. The horse is at plough. The rifle
> Returns to the chimney crotch and the hunter's hand.
> And nothing else than this? Was it for this
> That on an April day we stacked our arms
> Obedient to a soldier's trust? To lie
> Ground by heels of little men,
> Forever maimed, defeated, lost, impugned?
> And was I then betrayed? Did I betray?
>
> If it were said, as still it might be said—
> If it were said, and a word should run like fire,
> Like living fire into the roots of grass,
> The sunken flag would kindle on wild hills,

> The brooding hearts would waken, and the dream
> Stir like a crippled phantom under the pines,
> And this torn earth would quicken into shouting
> Beneath the feet of ragged bands—

>   The pen
> Turns to the waiting page, the sword
> Bows to the rust that cankers and the silence.

The idea of Lee's telling all he knows about the Civil War and the terms of surrender under which "we stacked out arms/ Obedient to a soldier's trust" commands his attention for a fleeting moment because he could perhaps restore the confidence and the self-respect of his "bound and trampled" people in this time of "shame and torment." But he pushes the thought out of his mind because his beloved land is now at peace, a troubled peace to be sure; but even an almost intolerable peace is better than war. The Blue Ridge is now "crowned with a haze of light" rather than submerged under a cloud of battle smoke. The "Shenandoah is golden with new grain," the "horse is at plough," the rifle is used for food and sport, and the "weeping of young women/ Rises no more." But even these evidences of physical well-being cannot completely satisfy a man of honor. Should he compromise principle for material comfort and "lie/ Ground by heels of little men" when everything he values seems "Forever maimed, defeated, lost, impugned"?

Then a most disturbing thought crosses Lee's mind, an idea so painful that he immediately considers another course of action: "And was I then betrayed? Did I betray?" He does not fully consider these questions now—he will return to them later—but his consciousness of them leads him to contemplate briefly what might happen if he were to abandon his policy of silence and patience:

> If it were said, as still it might be said—
> If it were said, and a word should run like fire,
> Like living fire into the roots of grass,
> The sunken flag would kindle on wild hills.

Even a word from him, he realizes, would be enough to have the young men like those who had greeted him so reverently on the steps take up their guns and resume the war. But since that disaster must be avoided, he attempts to focus his attention on the task at hand. Try as he may, however, he cannot clear his mind; he is too deeply conscious of his responsibility to these young students of Washington College and to the

thousands of others in the South—young and old, men and women—
who have placed their faith in him.

He returns to the questions he had pondered briefly a moment
before: "And was I then betrayed? Did I betray?" These meditations
comprise the fourth section of the poem:

> Among these boys whose eyes lift up to mine
> Within gray walls where droning wasps repeat
> A hollow reveille, I still must face,
> Day after day, the courier with his summons
> Once more to surrender, now to surrender all.
> Without arms or men I stand, but with knowledge only
> I fear what long I saw, before others knew,
> When Pickett's men streamed back, and I heard the tangled
> Cry of the Wilderness wounded, bloody with doom.
>
> The mountains, once I said, in the little room
> At Richmond, by the huddled fire, but still
> The President shook his head. The mountains wait,
> I said, in the long beat and rattle of siege
> At cratered Petersburg. Too late
> We sought the mountains and those people came.
> And Lee is in mountains now, beyond Appomattox,
> Listening long for voices that never will speak
> Again; hearing the hoofbeats come and go and fade
> Without a stop, without a brown hand lifting
> The tent-flap, or a bugle call at dawn,
> Or ever on the long white road the flag
> Of Jackson's quick brigades. I am alone,
> Trapped, consenting, taken at last in mountains.

The two parts of the question ("And was I then betrayed? Did I
betray?") give unity to this section. Many times in the days after the
war, the poet suggests, Lee must have recognized that the terms of
surrender accepted at Appomattox had been unrealistic. He was misled
by his own sense of honesty and justice, and the enemy had not
fulfilled the just and humane terms of surrender as evidenced by the
radical Reconstructionists. Lee fears, too, that he might have failed to
justify the trust placed in him by his followers. Should he have insisted,
as he had suggested to President Jefferson Davis, that he be allowed to
withdraw his forces to the mountains and make the enemy seek him
out? Among the most unpleasant of his memories is his recollection
that he saw the disastrous conclusion of the war before the others did;
and he strongly and sadly suspects he could have altered its course.[20]

Small bands of guerrilla warriors could have prolonged the war almost endlessly; perhaps the enemy could have been plagued and molested until his desire for peace was genuine.

Lee's dilemma becomes forcefully clear. Although he knows that the physical surrender at Appomattox was honorable, the conditions to which he must now submit are not. He is "alone/ Trapped, consenting, taken at last in mountains"; now he must "surrender all." Now he has neither arms nor men, but he has knowledge. As he listens "long for voices that never will speak / Again," he knows in his aloneness that he must struggle continuously to keep from surrendering his dignity as a human being. In silence and with patience he must find a way to act honorably and not abnegate his responsibility to those who are young enough to await a time when one will not forever be ground down under the "heels of little men."

As Lee's attitude hovers dangerously near despair, his thoughts are again disturbed, this time by the chapel bell announcing the daily devotions. Now not the bugle nor the rolling drum announces the impending battle, but the chapel bell "recalls the lonely mind," and Lee formulates the remarks he must give to the students who are looking to him for inspiration and guidance. The phrase "now to surrender all" links the fourth section to the concluding section, but in this final section the tone is not of dejection and despair; instead, the poem ends on a strong note of reconciliation and acceptance. His surrender, now final and complete, is the devotional act of the Christian who gives himself completely to God with the assurance that He will never forsake "His children and His children's children forever/ Unto all generations of the faithful heart":

> It is not the bugle now, or the long roll beating
> The simple stroke of a chapel bell forbids
> The hurtling dream, recalls the lonely mind.
> Young men, the God of your fathers is a just
> And merciful God Who in this blood once shed
> On your green altars measures out all days,
> And measures out the grace
> Whereby alone we live;
> And in His might He waits,
> Brooding within the certitude of time,
> To bring this lost forsaken valor
> And the fierce faith undying
> And the love quenchless
> To flower among the hills to which we cleave,

To fruit upon the mountains whither we flee,
Never forsaking, never denying
His children and His children's children forever
Unto all generations of the faithful heart.

III   New Praise and Old Remembrance

The title of Davidson's fourth volume of poetry, *The Long Street,* repeats the poet's image of Southern industrial development, his symbol of modern urban existence. This collection contains thirty-five pieces, of which more than a dozen go back to the 1920's, several were written in the 1930's and 1940's, but more than half are more recent. In technique, some of the latest poems are among Davidson's best. They demonstrate the master craftsmanship that one associates with the author of *The Tall Men* and "Lee in the Mountains": a sure ear for sound and rhythmic cadence; a simple, direct, straightforward, yet elegant, diction that reflects the poets's lifelong interest in the Roman and Greek classics; and a stately, or dignified, line devoid of esoteric vocabulary and erudite references. The poetic forms vary considerably. "Old Sailor's Choice" is written in verse paragraphs of varying lengths, some rhymed and some unrhymed. "The Case of Motorman 17" is verse drama; "The Gradual of the Northern Summer," also in verse paragraphs, is composed of strongly rhymed couplets; "A Touch of Snow" has a carefully controlled stanza pattern and a regular rhyme scheme. "Meditation on Literary Fame" approximates the form of Pindar's Epinician odes. With their flavor of the folk ballad, some of the brief narratives—"Fiddler Dow," "Joe Clisby," and "The Old Man of Thorn"—demonstrate the poet's nearness to his folk heritage.

But even with these impressive technical qualities, these poems are in no way contrived. In the carefully molded lines there is always an intensity of feeling that comes from an inner integrity and from a strictly defined set of sincere convictions. The momentary lapses into near cynicism, apparent in some of the poems in the *Lee* volume, are gone; but the irony, grave and stern, remains. It is evident, too, in these poems that Davidson has avoided the "guarded style," against which he cautioned his fellow poets in "Poetry as Tradition." He not only has sincere convictions, but he employs his poems as vehicles to carry these beliefs. He had warned his readers of the dangers of the poet's isolating himself from his community—of writing esoteric and sophisticated poetry intended for the perusal of none except his fellow artists. This practice, he insisted, would assure the demise of poetry and the destruction of society. This verse, with its simplicity and elegance of diction and its direct, forceful assertiveness, is written in a most "unguarded" style.

The Long Street is divided into five parts: (1) Northern Summers, Southern Autumns; (2) What City . . . What Land . . .?; (3) Joe Clisby; (4) The Case of Motorman 17; and (5) Fugitive Days. The poems in the first section reflect Davidson's experiences around Bread Loaf, Vermont, where he maintained a summer home for more than thirty years. The poet's love for New England is barely exceeded by his attachment to the South, and the reasons for his affection are not concealed. As Davidson had demonstrated in his most widely anthologized essay, "Still Rebels, Still Yankees," written almost thirty years before this book was published, these two regions have at least one thing in common: they have both struggled to prevent their rural mores from being completely destroyed by the twin gods of industry and progress.

The later poems reveal a restraint and tolerance not always present in the earlier verse. Although Davidson is quick to suggest the error of man's deserting his traditional heritage, there is no bitterness; instead, the poet seems to hope that some of the foolish will yet see the way. Some will realize that we still need the kind of education once given in the community schoolhouse:

> Whatever an empty schoolhouse still can teach
> We need to learn, and that is why we come
> So late and shy when you are not at home.
>
> We may be more than forty years too late
> To hear the last bell ringing near this gate
> And write the morning maxim on a slate,
>
> Yet have excuses you might not impeach:
> Problems that flare out like a comet's tail,
> Unsolved equations, surded with bane and bale.
>
> We do not shun your austere reprimand.
> Truant from glass-front life-adjustment schools
> Where Dunce and Master sit on equal stools,
> We seek a hand to guide a hand.[21]

But few remain who know what education is or what its purposes and uses are:

> Few now are left who know the ancient rule
> That tame abstract must wed the wild particular
> In school or art, but most of all in school,
> Else learning's spent to gild a fool

At market, altar, bench, or bar.
The shudder in the nerves must ever vex
Trim certainties of the vast complex,
And ever the wildcat's scream
Must break the Platonic dream
Else we but skim realities
And mock the great humanities.
To know this secret, you were not the first,
And will not be the last, we hope, to pledge
Redemption if the worst should come to worst,
And bring the schoolhouse back
Somewhere close to a wildcat's track
And the forest's finite edge.

One of Davidson's favorite themes is modern man's dissociation, his alienation from his tradition, and his lack of concern about the dissolution of his society. Surely anyone with the kind of education Davidson describes would be able to read the natural signs, to perceive recurring patterns, and to anticipate catastrophes that always follow certain occurrences. But most men are as complacent as the two painters in "A Touch of Snow" who disregard the natural signs indicating that summer is over and that the bad weather of winter is just ahead. The Poet who interprets the seasonal signs for them, asks, "Won't there be snow high up when the fog lifts?" But they are not concerned; the weather is fine now, and besides they can paint under the porch if the rain should come. One painter replies: "Oh, never mind the ridge . . . long as we may/ Keep summer here below." It is a man's nature, the poet suggests, to be oblivious to the future as long as things *seem* to be all right in the present. But the poet must warn them and lament that they are not wise enough to sense the impending danger facing the Western world.

Some of Davidson's most distinguished poetry is included in the second section of *The Long Street,* "What City . . . What Land?" The title is reminiscent of the passage in the *Aeneid* when Aeneas and his followers first view Carthage, the great city constructed by Dido. A wanderer forced to seek a new home after the fall of Troy, Aeneas becomes a kind of patron saint for the settlers of the South (both Tate and Andrew Lytle have used him in this role); and the fall of Troy becomes associated with the defeat of the Southern civilization. "Lines Written for Allen Tate on His Sixtieth Anniversary" opens in this way:

The sound of guns from beleaguered Donelson
Up river flowed to Benfolly's hearth.

> Year to familiar year we had heard it run
> World-round and back, till Lytle cried out: "Earth
> Is good, but better is land, and best
> A land still fought-for, even in retreat;
> For how else can Aeneas find his rest
> And the child hearken and dream at his grandsire's feet?"

As Aeneas turns from the ruins of Troy to find and establish a new home for his people, Davidson and his fellow Agrarians are concerned with "building a city." Although defeat seems almost certain, they must continue to struggle; for, like Aeneas, they can find rest in no other way. The poet is not suggesting that the heroic days of the Old South are recoverable as much as he is urging the faithful to attempt to preserve their integrity and their sense of individual human dignity amid the senseless clutter of modern living.

"Old Sailor's Choice" concerns the decisions man must make if he is to avoid the dehumanization of modern society. A present-day Ulysses relates how he has journeyed to hell and beyond—how he has been subjected to the monstrous dangers of Scylla and Charybdis. Scylla is described as a modern welfare state:

> Within her cliffs of sheer synthetic rock
> She glides on steely pathways. Plastic walls
> Checkered in pseudo-marble cavern her lair.
> These throw you off guard. "How," you ask,
> "Can anything go wrong where all is right—
> Rectangular, slide-ruled, and functional?"
> Mercy, pity, peace can be manufactured.
> Scylla can end your pain
> Now that the state decrees a tax increase
> And no one can complain.
> The neat-cut stencil echoes the brisk type.
> Machines do the rest. The postage is metered.
> And there is your release:
> Well-packaged, mercy, pity, peace.
> And I say the stretching neck and the grinning teeth
> In the soundproof room where artificial daylight
> Blacks out the scudding clouds and the churning storm-wrack,
> And the secretary with half-naked breasts
> Extends the telephone on a crimson claw
> And murmurs *Washington is calling!*

Despite Circe's advice, the modern Ulysses decides to choose Charybdis, even as the sorcerer bellows: "Not Charybdis! You have no choice! Trust Scylla . . . " Almost immediately, he finds himself alone in a turbulent sea:

> For Charybdis and the heaved insensuate sea
> Where nothing human dwells
> Take no deceitful shape, no monstrous face.
> There the vortex spins like Poe's own maelstrom.
> But a man's courage wears out the night.
> The hurricane howls, but carries off the dead.

After being tossed and heaved all night, he still would not choose Scylla, although she "is definitely human/ With various honorary degrees/ From the best institutions,/ And the world is at her knees." Suddenly it seems as if the "keel and mast" to which he had been clinging will be spun to the bottom of the sea. But, with a maximum of effort, Ulysses is able to save himself:

> Then leaped from the wash and clutched a lonely fig-tree
> Better than the trunk and the brine slashing,
> The tendons stretching, the ache in the deep marrow,
> And my fingers alive, clasping a wholesome thing.
> As the fig-tree roots clutched rock, so clutched I fig-tree
> And overhung Charybdis only by hand-hold
> Until the great suck stopped, and my mast and keel
> Easily swam beneath, and I could drop.
> There was timber enough for a raft
> And the naked truth of a man with salt in his beard.

The choice this modern Ulysses has made is extremely hazardous, but it is his only one if he wishes to maintain his individual freedom. Scylla demands nothing less than man's complete dehumanization—that he becomes a voiceless, thoughtless member of the Great Society. The man of courage, who insists that he will be an individual and not an automaton, may also be able to save himself by clutching a fig-tree.

In "Meditation on Literary Fame" Davidson returns to a theme he had treated in "Yeats and the Centaur," an essay in which he presents his views on the relationship that should exist between popular lore and the most sophisticated creations of the literary artist. Ideally, he writes, there should be no gap between "low" or folk art and "high" or literary art:

The popular lore ought to pass readily and naturally into the art; it ought not to have to be sought out by specialists in special corners, collected, edited, published, and reviewed; and then, perhaps only through some accident of taste or fashion, be appropriated, at long range, by a very literary poet. The reverse of the process ought also to work naturally and not at a forbidding long range. The art ought to pass readily into the popular lore, and not remain eternally aloof or difficult. Unless both processes continue in mutual interchange, society as well as art is in a bad state of health; but the bad health of society is a cause, not a result, of this unfavorable relationship.[22]

Davidson had long insisted that the poet must not withdraw from his society; instead, he should "retire more deeply within the body of the tradition to some point where he can utter himself with the greatest consciousness of his dignity as artist."[23] The society that has become completely secularized, that is fluid and unstable, that has accepted the dominance of science and is indisposed to accept poetry as truth—that society must inevitably relegate the poet to a position of no importance. When the poet understands that his creations are regarded as trifling, he withdraws from society; and his poetry becomes esoteric, personal, and subjective. The further a poet becomes separated from his society, the greater the distance between him and his proper subjects.

"Meditation on Literary Fame" is a tribute to a poet who is not dissociated, who has not become so detached and intellectualized that he must adopt the "guarded style":

> What net, what oar, what forest path or dream
> Retrieved for you, for us, the Theban lyre?
> The Scholiast from Byzantium's funeral gleam
> Plucked but the mute, the shattered frame;
> And Yeats, consorting with moon-demons, heard
> Images only, clutched at the abstract Bird
> Of charred philosophy until he lost
> Usheen, whom once he knew, and his dear land,
> And all the Celtic host.
> Fleeing that bitter choice, your reverend great-grandsire
> Sailed, where the Muses led, to this Western strand.

In the opening lines the poet asks the question to which he will devote his attention for the remainder of the poem: "What net, what oar, what forest path or dream/ Retrieved for you, for us, the Theban Lyre?" An earlier draft of this poem included in the title "An Epinician Ode," which indicates that the poet is presenting a tribute such as Pindar offered to commemorate victory in the great games. This tribute goes to a fellow poet who has "retrieved" the lyre of Pindar, an instrument upon which it was said the Theban, because he maintained an especially close relationship with the gods, could play better than any of his contemporaries. The real benefactors, the speaker informs the poet, are those of us who know the products of the poet's creative genius.

The dry-as-dust scholars who preserved the texts of some of the Pindaric Odes, glossed, annotated, and often corrupted them, had no genuine appreciation of the art with which they were dealing. They did not "retrieve" the lyre; they "plucked but the mute, the shattered frame." Neither was Yeats able to assimilate the gift of the immortal ancient poet, although his mistake was not that of the scholar. He "clutched at the abstract Bird/ Of charred philosophy until he lost/ Usheen, whom once he knew, and his dear land,/ And all the Celtic host." In "Yeats and the Centaur" Davidson argues that the Irish poet became too self-conscious in his use of his native materials:

The early Yeats wrote ballads, like the "Ballad of the Fox-hunter" and the "Ballad of Father Gilligan," and folk songs, or quasi-folk songs, like "Down by the Valley Gardens." He also wrote "The Wanderings of Usheen," a semiepical poem, and composed lyrics and plays that utilized the ancient Irish myths. . . . Then, after a time, the poetry ceased to be narrative or in any way "folkish." The myths and popular lore become occasional references, or they become, in the modern sense, symbols, which are merged into the larger "frame of reference" established by the private mythology explained in *A Vision.*[24]

Yeats, who forsook his native land with its rich and ancient lore, made a symbolic voyage to Byzantium, the "golden city of the imagination where Unity of Being has permeated an entire culture."[25] In attempting to achieve immortality through the creation of a work of art, Yeats became too esoteric and subjective and "lost/ Usheen, whom once he knew, and his dear land,/ And all the Celtic host."

The poet's ancestors, the speaker reminds his fellow bard to whom he is presenting this ode of victory, avoided that "bitter choice" and followed the Muses to a new land:

> Where you were born, exiled Olympian song
> Ever companioned us in game or chase.
> For how could poet rightly shape his tongue
> To cheer the winner of a country race
> Unless some God or Goddess had stood there,
> Likeness of Mentor in a hunter's coat,
> And tuned the winged wands for us,
> And whetted on the praise?
> By Isis or the Thames you found none fabulous
> As those proud men at any country fair
> Who wore the Southern Gray or Tennessee butternut
> As if great Pindar sat in the Judge's chair.

The poet being honored possesses *fortunatus,* the knowledge that makes men "blessed":

> It *[fortunatus]* rests upon traditional religion—or, in Vergil's exact language, "the rustic gods, Pan and old Silvanus, and the sister Nymphs," which I have freely translated "The God of his fathers." It is a knowledge that possesses the heart rather than a knowledge achieved merely by the head—a knowledge that pervades the entire beings. . . it establishes the blessed man in a position where economic use, enjoyment, understanding, and religious reverence are not separated but are fused in one.[26]

Because this poet does not suffer from the modern disease of the dissociated sensibility, there is no separation of the heart and the head. A "blessed" man, he has retained a firm belief in "the God of his fathers"; consequently, he does not have to go off in search of a holy city. He has found his proper place among his people; he does not attempt to separate himself from them or to live counter to them. In Oxford, London, Byzantium, or nowhere else has he found any so "fabulous/ As those proud men at any country fair/ Who wore the Southern Gray or Tennessee butternut."

Despite the evidence that seems to point to a contrary conclusion, the poem ends with a proclamation of victory:

> Then let my messenger, this song, evoke
> New praise and old remembrance like the voice
> That first we heard beneath your Talking Oak
> Foretelling your best victory—
> (What if it's called defeat, this later year!)
>   *Where are no griefs, can be no joys!*
>   *Happy the land where men hold dear*
>   *Myth that is truest memory,*
>   *Prophecy that is poetry.*

The early poems, those of the early and mid-1920's, were written before Davidson became fully aware of his deep and abiding affection for the South. Then the poet began his journey down the Long Street: first, in *The Tall Men* into his Southern heritage; then, in *Lee in the Mountains and Other Poems,* into the legacy of the Civil War. Most of the later poems were written after the Agrarian phase and after Davidson had lost all hopes of preserving the social and cultural forms of the Old South. But the tone of these later poems is not bitter; instead, there is a carryover of the affirmation of faith and the plea for truth and justice that permeate the final section of "Lee in the Mountains."

In these later poems, as in all of his poetry after *An Outland Piper,* Davidson avoids the "guarded style" which he describes and cautions against in "Poetry as Tradition." One of his purposes is to restore to poetry its social function: to serve as "messenger" to his people and to "evoke/ New praise and old remembrance." He attempts to recapitulate the past in order to make his readers mindful of their heritage, that "vast continuum of human experience" which is known as tradition, and of the forces in the modern regime that have already relegated the poet to a position of no importance and that seem intent upon the destruction of civilization itself. To fulfill his traditional role, the poet must sing of experiences that he shares with his fellow man. He must develop neither a set of ideas nor a personal style that is peculiar to himself. As a responsible and respected member of society, he must "share in the general concern as to the conditions of life"; he must "bear the brunt of the battle against the common foe."[27] Poetry should be a means of communication, and its "meaning" should not be beyond the reach of the reasonably alert and inquisitive reader. At times in his role of bard and prophet, Davidson's argument becomes so obtrusive that the poem suffers. But, in the best of his verse, the totality of his vision, the range of his imagination, and the force and clarity of his presentation give him a place almost unique among his contemporaries.

CHAPTER 5

The Poet as Prophet

I Beginnings as a Critic

WHETHER Davidson's reputation will rest primarily upon his achievements as a poet or as an essayist is not certain. While his best creative periods for poetry were occasional, prose was a dominant form of expression throughout his career as a literary critic and as a social and political philosopher, historian, scholar of native traditions, and rhetorician. One thing is certain—his prose, of a remarkably even quality, is distinguished by stylistic grace and persuasive logic. In one sense, poetry is easier to write because, as Davidson noted, "poetry is that form of statement which does not require or even imply proof."[1] Convincing prose, on the other hand, demands cogent reasoning and demonstrated authority, both of which characterize his work. Critics have often taken note of his "mastery of style and incisiveness of expression,"[2] and one has written that "His prose is not merely correct, it is lucid, smooth, supple; few Americans have a more carefully chiseled style, agreeable to the eye and ear without trumpery ornamentation, clear to the understanding without falling into puerility."[3]

Most of Davidson's essays were written in exploration and defense of Agrarianism and its principles; but his earliest pieces were literary criticisms and reviews, and such writings form a considerable share of his total work. During the duration of the publication of *The Fugitive* from April, 1922, to December, 1925, Davidson contributed one essay on "Certain Fallacies in Modern Poetry"—in which he denied the priority of a program, of an esthetic, or of a set of dogmatic rules in the creation of poetry in "the grand style"—and four reviews assessing works of T. S. Eliot, Archibald MacLeish, E. E. Cummings, Hervey Allen, and R. C. Trevelyan.[4]

The review of Eliot's *Homage to John Dryden* is of interest for Davidson's recognition of several points of agreement between the theories of Eliot and the Fugitives. The central theme of Davidson's other reviews of his contemporaries is expressed in the third: "given a rather chaotic modern world, disturbing in its complexity, and along with it the traditional instruments of the poet, how shall the poet orient himself, and what bearing will the bewildering condition of the cosmos have on his thought and on his form?" This problem vexed Davidson at the moment in his own creative work, and he did not resolve it to his particular satisfaction until the writing of *The Tall Men* when he discovered that the narrative form and the use of his region's historic past proved to be fruitful orientations from which to make a statement about the human condition.

During the life of *The Fugitive*, Davidson also contributed reviews to *The Guardian*, a lively but short-lived little review published in Philadelphia; but his first sustained piece of criticism was his essay, "Joseph Conrad's Directed Indirections," for the *Sewanee Review*. Davidson had worked out his major ideas for this essay in his master's thesis for Vanderbilt University, "The Inversive Method of Narration in the Novels and Stories of Joseph Conrad," directed by John Crowe Ransom and completed in May 1922. Writing shortly after Conrad's death and at a time when his critical reputation was eclipsed by a talented new generation of writers, such as James Joyce and Virginia Woolf, Davidson was among the earliest to treat in definitive terms one of the major complexities of Conrad's style.

Davidson recognizes Conrad's calculated and strategic manipulation of time and chronology as an organic technique in the novel and as a method of reducing emphasis on plot and action and of increasing the reader's interest in the subtleties of mood and character psychology. This tactic—which Davidson labels the "inversive method"—"eliminated the meaner elements which in the history of fiction have so often operated to hold the novel down to cheap and mechanical formulas; it brings into emphasis the inner forces which should dignify great narrative art; it puts a thoughtful cast on the face of melodrama itself."[5]

Davidson—making an unusual use of his knowledge of Conrad, and applying his own critical imagination—entered in 1925 a contest sponsored by the *Saturday Review of Literature* for the best suggested endings to Conrad's unfinished novel *Suspense*. His entry, which won fourth prize, was based upon an extension of the typical ending for a Conrad novel in which the hero goes down to defeat but is still faithful to a concept of dignity superior to the impersonal antagonistic forces which destroy him—"a kind of residue of loyalty that remains untainted by fate."[6]

The proving ground for the formulation of Davidson's emerging critical and cultural theories was the book page he edited for the Nashville *Tennessean* newspaper between February, 1924, and November, 1930. As early as August 22, 1923, Davidson had considered suggesting a column on poetry for the Nashville papers, as an extension of the Fugitive group activity, "or a real honest-to-goodness weekly literary column, such as they ought to have,—or even a page."[7] Thus, when the managing editor of the *Tennessean* offered Davidson in January, 1924, a position as editor of a weekly literary page, he welcomed not only the opportunity of having a forum for his opinions but also the additional supplement it provided to his slender pre-Depression salary as an instructor at Vanderbilt—and the free books.

Beginning on February 10, 1924, with a full page and his own column of literary commentary and book reviews, Davidson drew from the ranks of fellow Fugitives and academics for his reviewers at first and later more heavily from local journalists and townspeople. During the page's existence, among its contributors were John Crowe Ransom, Allen Tate, Stanley Johnson, Cleanth Brooks, Walter Clyde Curry, Stanley Horn, Arthur Palmer Hudson, Andrew Lytle, Edwin Mims, Frank L. Owsley, Edd Winfield Parks, John Donald Wade, and Robert Penn Warren—a rich cross-section of American scholars, critics, poets, historians, and writers of fiction.[8]

When Davidson threatened to resign in 1928 because the *Tennessean* refused to put the page on a respectable financial footing, the owner and publisher, Colonel Luke Lea, countered by offering to syndicate the page to papers in Memphis and Knoxville and to give the editor a considerable raise. Davidson set to work again with renewed enthusiasm to make his page, as he wrote Allen Tate, "the most substantial and distinctive thing of its kind in the South and in the United States if possible."[9] That he succeeded is indicated by the plaudits he began to receive in the pages of critical quarterlies, such as Ernest Hartsock's statement in the *Sewanee Review* that Davidson had become "an active force in our literary life,"[10] and Howard Mumford Jones's designation in the *Virginia Quarterly Review* of his book-reviewing as "brilliantly done."[11] When the page fell victim to the Depression in November, 1930, just as it had reached its height of influence, many New York publishers wrote to express their protest and regret.

Of greatest importance to the development of Davidson's mind was the great body of literature he read during the years of his editorship. In about seven years of reviewing, Davidson assessed over three hundred and seventy books by such novelists as Sherwood Anderson, Louis Bromfield, James Branch Cabell, Willa Cather, Joseph Conrad, Theodore Dreiser, John Dos Passos, William Faulkner, Ellen Glasgow, Ernest Hemingway, Sinclair Lewis, Thomas Mann, and Thomas Wolfe; poets such as Conrad Aiken, Hart Crane, E. E. Cummings, T. S. Eliot, Robert Frost, Amy Lowell, Ransom and Tate; historians Charles A. Beard, Claude G. Bowers, V. L. Parrington, and Ulrich B. Phillips; social and literary critics James Truslow Adams, Ralph Borsodi, Van Wyck Brooks, Henry Seidel Canby, Joseph Wood Krutch, Bertrand Russell, and George Bernard Shaw.[12] In all, the reviews provide a rich chronicle of the last half of a powerfully productive, influential decade in American letters; and Davidson reflects in the majority of them an acute and dependable critical intelligence, and a sense of judgment which the passage of time has impressively verified.[13]

In working out his critical standards, Davidson also gave earliest expression to a theory which informs much of his social and literary criticism—the necessity for harmony between the artist and the region from which he draws his subject matter. Writing in condemnation of the work of T. S. Stribling, Davidson notes that "It is an easy trick to make an arbitrary arrangement of sensational features and call the result fiction. The writers of syndicated 'sob-stuff' and high-life scandals understand that trick perfectly. It is another and a more difficult thing to plumb a people to the depth in the search for the essentials by which they live, and then to give these the clear, fully-rounded representation of art, with complete respect to every individual, whether noble or ignominious."[14] Thus, among Southern novelists, Stark Young elicits Davidson's praise because he is one of the few "who sees the Southern way of life as a whole and communicates it with the grace and conviction that it deserves." Davidson feels however, that Thomas Wolfe, though a superb and talented virtuoso, was unable to inform *Look Homeward, Angel* with control and conviction because he was at odds with his environment. "Or to put it differently," Davidson writes, "there is evidently no real harmony between this artist and the materials he deals with; and the result is inevitably a kind of inner confusion, which, though it does not destroy the incidental merits of the book, does hurt its total effect."[15]

Davidson worked this idea out in a fuller way in his article "The Artist as Southerner" written for the *Saturday Review of Literature* in 1926.[16] The writer who lives south of the Mason-Dixon Line is torn between two approaches to the use of regional materials—the remote, austere approach of the uninhibited modern, or the emptily provincial approach of the inferior writers who have "mooned over the Lost Cause and exploited the hard-dying sentimentalism of antebellum days." The Old South, Davidson notes, "left no culture of ideas that the Southern writer can cheerfully use; he can no more accommodate himself to its fabric than a flapper can put on hoopskirts. And in the new order his situation is equally baffling. He sees industrialism marching on, and can digest the victorious cries of civic boosters even less readily than the treacly lamentations of the old school."

Given this dilemma, the successful writer is one who can resist dissociation from his environment and move in his art from the particular to the universal. The truly "autochthonous" writer does not feel the division of his age:

Frost in New England, Hardy in Wessex, Hamsun and Bojer in Europe are all autochthonous writers in the best meaning of the term. They are, literally speaking, of the same time and place with their generation and section, and, whatever their superiority as geniuses, they are not detached from men's fundamental thoughts and feelings. Local materials come to them as fresh and immediate themes, to which they can easily give a character of the universal rather than the merely provincial, and they are not plagued with inhibitions.

Thus, Davidson concluded, "to be Southern should mean much to any writer who has had the courage and endurance to remain in his country and fight the battle out." That many Southern writers did exactly that is evidenced by what has come to be called "the Southern literary renaissance" which swamped the literary marketplace in the following decades.

These ideas would prove especially fruitful for Davidson the artist in the working out of his own esthetic, but they were also helpful in the formulation of an attitude towards his time and place which would eventuate in the assumption of a position of leadership among a group of Southern writers who were soon to take a stand as Agrarians against the impersonal forces of the industrial age. But, before they published their symposium *I'll Take My Stand* in 1930, and Davidson became the chief expositor of Agrarianism, he had formulated in capsule in some of his reviews a few of his basic Agrarian principles. The occasions were assessments of such books as Frank L. Owsley's *State Rights in the Confederacy,* Ulrich B. Phillips' *Life and Labor in the Old South,* Claude Bowers' *The Tragic Era,* Walter L. Fleming's *The Sequel of Appomattox,* James Truslow Adams' *Our Business Civilization,* and

Ralph Borsodi's *This Ugly Civilization*—books which were circulating among Davidson's friends who were to pass with him from the Fugitive to the Agrarian fellowship and which supported their growing convictions about the ills of the age and their cure.

In defining the function of a "provincial" book reviewer, Davidson distinguishes in 1928 between the kind of provincialism he had condemned in his *Saturday Review* article and a new kind which could help save the South. The wrong kind is "known by its closed mind or its limited experience or both; it has generally too much self-sufficiency and swagger; it is noisy and egotistical." But the other sort is "a kind of provincialism that is allied to the self-reliance of Emerson's teaching and to the 'know thyself' of the ancient sages," which Davidson wishes to rescue from derogatory connotations: "A modest amount of provincialism, in fact, becomes almost a necessity, if we are to have any peace of mind and fruitful repose. Provincialism, in the favorable sense I am thinking about, is a philosophy of life that begins with one's own rooftree. It is rebellious against the modern principle of standardization, as it is carried over from science and machinery into habits of thought.[17] This statement illustrates the early basic antagonism of the natural and technological attitudes—Agrarianism verses industrialism. Other statements critical of the influence of Northern capitalism and industrialism are scattered throughout reviews:

At this moment when industrialism is sweeping down upon them, and Northern capital is resuming the process of conquest which Grant and Sherman never, thank Heaven, fully completed; Southerners need to examine their great heritage before they commit themselves beyond retraction to the processes of the machine age.[18] (1927)

For the rulership of business never can be an enlightened one, because business exists only by Profit. Whatever charities or high-minded promotions business may indulge in, its final concern must be with Profit. Therefore, its entire view of government, art, religion, education, whatever-you-please, is found to be colored by a basically selfish philosophy.[19] (1929)

The World War was the first war in history to be thoroughly mechanized, on a fully modern, presumably "efficient" basis. It was also the first war in all history to produce no great generals, no great leaders, and perhaps not a single piece of first-class strategy. In other words, the triumph of the machine![20] (1930)

In one passage there is an affirmation of Davidson's belief that modern man must assert his mastery and control over economic forces instead of placidly accepting as inevitable whatever technology brings: "If there is no human control of society, if everything depends on vast economic forces that automatically and anonymously make everything happen, it is useless to go to history for lessons as to conduct. For the 'forces' act, whether we will or no, and we had just as well save our strength and sit around and wait for the forces to do their stuff"[21] (1929).

Instead of such surrender, Davidson recommends a course of positive action by holding onto the traditions and lessons of history: "we must recover the past, or at least in some way realize it, in order that we may bring the most genuine and essential parts of our own tradition forward in contact with the inevitable new tradition now in process of formation. Only thus can we achieve vital continuity in the national life"[22] (1928).

Davidson and the later Agrarians felt that the chief instruments of science and technology were opposed to the esthetic life; as a result, the application of scientific behaviorism to literature was bound to be stifling. A most interesting critique of such an approach is Davidson's charge that Hemingway's *A Farewell to Arms* is a perfect example of an effort to combine the role of artist and behavioral scientist:

Mr. Hemingway here is playing scientist, and he is watching people behave. It is a mistake to suppose that people behave morally or immorally, becomingly or unbecomingly. . . . There is no good, no ill, no pretty, no ugly—only behavior. Behaviorism argues that there is stimulus and response, nothing else, and Mr. Hemingway's books contain (ostensibly, but not quite) nothing else. The novel is a bold and exceptionally brilliant attempt to apply scientific method to art, and I devoutly hope that all the scientists will read it and admire it immensely.[23] (1929)

When Allen Tate objected that Davidson was not dealing with Hemingway fairly by the scientific association, he admitted that he had perhaps overstated the case: "I am afraid that I sacrificed Hemingway (to some extent) in order to make a point against science," he wrote Tate. "But I should add that I did this the more readily because I felt that he was exposed to criticism, at least to debate, on this particular point. I certainly respect him, and I'm glad to have your opinion of him to take to heart."[24]

Thus during the decade before *I'll Take My Stand* appeared in 1930, Davidson was gradually led into a serious study and evaluation of developments in American and Southern culture and history which provided excellent background for the more important tasks to come. There is no discernible line to be drawn between his early work as a Fugitive poet and critic and his later work as an Agrarian; for the motivating factor in both was his desire to understand the proper attitude of the artist toward his social environment.

II From Fugitive to Agrarian

The relationship between the Fugitive and Agrarian groups is frequently misunderstood by literary critics and historians who very often treat them as synonymous by using the hyphenated epithet "Fugitive-Agrarian writers."[25] The groups had, however, quite separate and distinctively different endeavors. As Louise Cowan notes, in her definitive literary history, *The Fugitive Group,* "The Fugitives were a quite tangible body of sixteen poets who, having no particular program, met frequently from 1915 to 1928 for the purpose of reading and discussing their own work. The Agrarians were twelve scholars of various disciplines who, from about 1928 to 1935, were united by common principle rather than contiguity and whose intercommunications were conducted, for the most part, through letters and essays."[26] Historically speaking, the only thing the two groups had in common was the membership of Davidson, Ransom, Tate, and Warren, the most talented and perceptive nuclei of both. In a deeper philosophical sense, however, the Agrarian movement for these four was in no sense a desertion of the cause of art and poetry for concerns that were social and political: for in both causes their positions as men of letter were preeminent.

What happened to them, Mrs. Cowan has written, "involved no real change in heart and character; instead it was a movement toward wholeness, toward accepting with their minds something they had known all along in their poetry."[27] And the fact that poetry was their chosen form of artistic expression is revelatory. "The composition of poetry is evidence," says Richard Weaver, that, for the poet, "values have a reality, and that he is capable of emotion upon the subject of value. . . . There is a minimal truth in even the wildest metaphor simply because the world is, from one point of view, a unitary thing . . . . The practice of poetry amounts in effect to a confession of faith in immanent reality, which is the gravest of all commitments."[28]

A commitment to poetry, in other words, is not an evasion of reality; instead, it is an attempt to discover in the physical world, by way of image and metaphor, those values which inform nature and life with meaning. Davidson affirmed Weaver's point during the discussions which occurred as a part of the Fugitives' Reunion at Vanderbilt University in May, 1956. When Merrill Moore tried to assert a complete separation between the poet and the politician, between the Fugitive and Agrarian, Davidson retorted: "I would say that the symposium *I'll Take My Stand* can be taken just as much as a defense of poetry as it can be taken as a defense of the South—or of any particular politics, or economics, or anything. The general point is—in that book—that in the order of life that we would defend or seek to establish, these things are not to be separated if life is to be healthy at all; that the separation of them into specialties under the modern regime is the thing, above everything else, that destroys poetry."[29] A relevant point was inserted in the same discussion at its conclusion by Louise Cowan: the four Fugitives who made poetry a primary pursuit and who devoted their lives to literature were the same four who committed themselves to an Agrarian program for reform.[30] The movements were indeed separate, but the social concerns of the Agrarians for a better way of life certainly were inspired by their equal concern for the life of the imagination.

Davidson's comment to Merrill Moore emphasized the universal nature of the relationship between the poet and society, which is indicative of the Agrarians' belief that the criticisms they made of society were meant for the welfare of the whole American community —not simply of the South. In the larger cultural perspective, of course, the Agrarians were in the spirit of many reform movements underway in this country and abroad that were elicited by increasingly precarious national economies and by the threatened loss of humane principles in the monolithic societies being created by the forces of industrialism and mechanization. By the 1920's, America had reached the peak of a wild, roller-coaster ride compelled by an irresponsible materialism; but the ride down the other side, instead of approaching another peak, plummeted into the dark passage of 1929, one full of the frightening horrors of a collapsed economy. Outwardly, America had been prosperous and successful, but inwardly its spiritual security was corrupt.

The Agrarians shared ideas with the American Populist and Progressive traditions in their efforts to protect the rights of the farmer in the national economy and in their concern for the welfare of the individual confronted by heartless industrial bureaucracy. Across the Atlantic, the Agrarians found an English counterpart to their program in the ideas of the Distributists led by Hilaire Belloc and G. K. Chesterton, and supported by T. S. Eliot. American distrust of mechanization had already been expressed in such works as Elmer Rice's drama *The Adding Machine* in 1923 (preceded a year earlier by an American production of Karel Capek's equally expressionistic and anti-industrial *R.U.R.*) and in the essays of Granville Hicks, Lewis Mumford, and Ralph Aiken. And not unrelated are the disillusionments and criticisms of American expatriates such as T. S. Eliot, Gertrude Stein, and Ernest Hemingway, who charged their homeland with failure to live according to its expressed ideals. Like Joseph Wood Krutch in *The Modern Temper* (1929), the Agrarians seriously questioned the assumption that modern man becomes wiser and happier in proportion to the ingenuity of the machinery which surrounds him.

The group with whom the Agrarians would have appeared to have a close affinity were the New Humanists, led by Professors Irving Babbitt and Paul Elmer More, who recommended a return to traditional values reflected in the art, literature, and humanistic studies of Western man. Reacting against the pessimistic influence of scientific determinism and naturalism in literature and philosophy, the New Humanists emphasized an ethical system which would restore man's ability to control his own destiny through the exercise of restraint and reason, especially as exemplified in the best that has been thought and written in the past.

While both the New Humanists and Agrarians deplored the state of modern culture, rejected the philosophy of "progress," and cherished esthetics, they disagreed about the actual utility of their proposed plans. The Humanists tried to deduce a view of life from literature instead of looking at life directly and suiting a plan of social action to fit reality; as a result, they were too intellectually abstract for the Agrarians. In a letter to Allen Tate, Davidson noted that the Humanists "simply offer to superimpose a vague scheme of art-criticism-education on a social system that is bound to reject it. . . ." Having just read portions of the Humanists' recently published *Humanism and America, Essays on the Outlook of Modern Civilization,* Davidson commented that "It's quite evident that they have some of our doctrines, so to speak embedded, but in the main they seem to write about Art and do not offer much real social thinking."[31]

In Davidson's own essay in *I'll Take My Stand,* he speaks more directly and eloquently about the Humanists' failing: "[They] commend us to Sophocles and God, *in vacuo.* Their thinking stops where it should begin, with social conditions that shape the artist's reaction. Like Arnold, they imagine that culture will conquer Philistinism and have faith that the 'best' ideas will prevail over the false ideas or no-ideas of the great Anarch. In Arnold's time it was reasonable to entertain such a hope. Today it is the academic equivalent of Y.M.C.A. 'leadership.' " [32] The two groups even came to public verbal blows when Humanist Robert Shafer published a personally abusive attack on Allen Tate, whose critical essay on "The Fallacy of Humanism" had appeared in the July, 1929, issue of *The Criterion*. [33]

While the Agrarians may be considered a part of the general dissatisfaction with the course of American culture, they were different in that they drew inspiration from a set of ideas which had been given a distinctively American expression by Thomas Jefferson, who wrote in his *Notes on Virginia* (1787) that "Those who labor in the Earth are the chosen people of God, if ever He had a chosen people, whose breasts he made His peculiar deposit for substantial and genuine virtue." To him the farming life contained the seat of virtue and the industrial, metropolitan life contained the seat of evil and corruption. The government, Jefferson believed, should reflect the interests of the property-owning yeoman farmer, free him from centralized authority, and preserve sectional individuality. The American economy of the twentieth century had done anything but protect the minority position of the farmer who lived what Jefferson and the Agrarians considered the "good life," one self-sufficient and free of the oppressive influence of industry and technology.

While expanding industrialism during the first three decades of the twentieth century drew the rural population into the metropolis, it also took advantage of those who remained on the farm by allowing them the smallest share possible in the nation's wealth. While the New Deal was to give the farmer a better advantage, it was to do so at the cost of local self-government and freedom from federal authority, losses of which neither the Agrarians nor Jefferson would approve. [34]

Other important American thinkers who obviously influenced the Agrarians were John Taylor (the brilliant social and political theorist and the entrenched foe of centralized federal authority) and John C. Calhoun (especially through his theory of concurrent majority). [35] And, as Randall Stewart suggested, "if *Walden* was the chief criticism of industrial America written in the Nineteenth Century, *I'll Take My Stand* is the chief criticism of the same subject to appear in this century." One demurrer should be entered, however. Unlike Thoreau and the Transcendentalists, the Agrarians did not hold that human nature was perfectible or that man, as Jefferson insisted, could construct a better and more highly organized society through his reason. The Nashville Agrarians assumed that man needed a stronger support than his own reason.

The most immediate historical and cultural event which provoked the Agrarians to act and write their book was the Scopes trial which had occurred in Dayton, Tennessee, in 1925. If one had to pick a date for the germination of *I'll Take My Stand,* Davidson said, "I think you'd pick 1925, when the Dayton trial set everything aflame."[36] A young science instructor named John Thomas Scopes had been persuaded to test the Butler Act, which said it was unlawful "to teach any theory that denies the story of the Divine Creation of man as taught in the Bible." When the ardent liberal Clarence Darrow was called in as counsel for the defense, when champion fundamentalist William Jennings Bryan announced he would join counsel for the prosecution, and when the popular press had blown the whole affair to preposterous proportions, the entire trial assumed the character of a symbolic struggle between the forces of science and religion, liberalism and conservatism, agnosticism and fundamentalism, technology and tradition.

No matter how one considered the trial, the South in the public view seemed on the side of ignorance, closed-mindedness, and backwardness; and the American populace had forced upon it the choice between Darwin and Moses, between faith and progress—a false choice which nevertheless impaled Southerners and Northerners alike on the horns of a dilemma. "I can hardly speak for others," Davidson wrote, "but for John Ransom and myself, surely, the Dayton episode dramatized, more ominously than any other event easily could, how difficult it was to be a Southerner in the twentieth century, and how much more difficult to be a Southerner and also a writer. It was horrifying to see the cause of liberal education argued in a Tennessee court by a famous agnostic lawyer from Illinois named Clarence Darrow. It was still more horrifying—and frightening—to realize that the South was being exposed to large-scale public detraction and did not know or much care how to answer."[37] Thus the poet was transformed into the conscious Southerner. "As in all cultural crises," Louise Cowan has rightly noted,

the turmoil issuing from the trial brought into the foreground ideas and attitudes that had been taken for granted in the past but that were now no longer generally accepted. An event which caused many intelligent Southerners to reject their native land propelled these four Fugitive poets into a careful study of Southern history. For the sake of honesty, they found themselves forced to defend in their native section characteristics which they knew to be unoffensive and even valuable and finally, from an understanding of the deeply religious structure of life in the Tennessee hills, a structure which had its expression in

Fundamentalism, grew the conviction which led these poets to their first overt defense of the South.[38]

Davidson spoke directly to the issue in two essays before *I'll Take My Stand* became a reality. Although he was not then and never became by any stretch of definition a fundamentalist believer in Christianity, he saw fundamentalism not necessarily as a narrow-minded faith but as an essential part of the traditional belief which gives order to the fabric of society.[39] In his 1926 essay on "The Artist as Southerner," he wrote that "Fundamentalism, in one aspect, is blind and belligerent ignorance; in another, it represents a fierce clinging to poetic supernaturalism against the encroachments of cold logic; it stands for moral seriousness."[40]

As a concluding article for a series interpreting the modern South to the nation at large, *Forum* magazine published Davidson's "First Fruits of Dayton" in which he reiterates the value of fundamentalism in the age of science and progress: "Fundamentalism, whatever its wild extravagances, is at least morally serious in a day when morals are treated with levity; and . . . it offers a sincere, though a narrow, solution to a major problem of our age: namely, how far science, which is determining our physical ways of life, shall be permitted also to determine our philosophy of life." Despite the sharp criticism received by Southern education since Dayton, Davidson outlines Southern advancements in this field, noting that antievolution statutes are simply "straw barriers against a great wind," after all, and "Whatever education can do, it will presently have an opportunity to do in the South."

Davidson's major concern in the essay is not *whether* the South has the potential for cultural progress, but *what* the nature of the "progress" is to be: "Whose ideal of progress is the South to follow?" Is it to be the ideal posited by the "New South" champions of materialism and technology and by the supporters of a national conformity in thought and social action? Obviously, industrialism and big business hold the keys for the future: "They are the lords and masters of the industrial expansion. . . . It is in their hands to cast the deciding vote in the matter of intellectual progress." Therefore, the business man must get in touch with the traditions of the South, not reject them as Dayton would compel him to do, because "only that ideal of progress is justified which affirms and does not destroy the local individuality and true characteristics of the South."

A regional integrity, a provincialism—which "means, not sectionalism, not insularity and bigotry of mind, but differentiation, which is a thoroughly ancient and honorable and American idea"—is as important for the state of the union as it is for the imagination of the artist: "for while we live under the blessing of national unity, we must take care that unity does not become uniformity."[41] This essay constitutes a full-scale dress-rehearsal for *I'll Take My Stand* in its early formulation of Davidson's basic feelings which led him to Agrarianism; however, his stand was firmer and less conciliatory than here.

III   In Defense of Agrarianism

The idea for the publication of a symposium, which eventuated in *I'll Take My Stand,* seems first to have been generated in 1926 in correspondence among Allen Tate, John Crowe Ransom, and Davidson.[42] The project assumed various forms over the following years, from a critical examination of Southern literature to a history of the South; and the circle of discussion and correspondence expanded to include other interested contributors, such as Frank L. Owsley, Andrew Lytle, and John Donald Wade. The bulk of the correspondence seems to have passed betwen Tate, who spent over a year in Paris on a Guggenheim grant between 1928 and 1930, and Davidson, who appears to have taken the largest share of initiative and responsibility in seeing the project through to completion.

While Tate served as a powerful intellectual influence and source of inspiration for the enthusiastic young Southerners involved in the book, Davidson carried out the necessary correspondence, gathered the essays as they were completed, handled all the local technical matters relating to the contract with Harper which Tate had negotiated in New York, and edited much of the manuscript. Tate later wrote that "Without his devotion and determination the symposium could not have been organized," and he has accorded Davidson the position of leader of this Agrarian effort.[43]

Because of Davidson's demonstrated authority in the field, his weekly reviews for the *Tennessean* book page, his extensive reading in regional literature, and his essays like "The Artist as Southerner" for the *Saturday Review of Literature,* Davidson assumed the task of writing for the symposium the essay on the place of literature and art in contemporary society. As Tate noted in one of the tentative tables of contents for the book, "he knows and understands it better than any of us."[44] In the general statement of principles with which the Agrarians introduced their volume, they noted, in the course of enumerating the unfortunate influences of industrialism on civilization, that the "arts [do not] have a proper life under industrialism, with the general decay of sensibility which attends it. Art depends, in general, like religion, on a right attitude to nature; and in particular on a free and disinterested observation of nature that occurs only in leisure. Neither the creation nor the understanding of works of art is possible in an industrial age except by some local and unlikely suspension of the industrial drive."[4 5] Davidson's essay, "A Mirror for Artists," is a fully developed argument for this succinctly stated point of view.

As he had observed in his earlier *Saturday Review* article, Davidson believes that an integral relationship exists between the production of art and the conditions of the artist's life. The kinds of societies in which art properly flourished in the past have been "societies which were for the most part stable, religious, and agrarian; where the goodness of life was measured by a scale of values having little to do with the material values of industrialism; where men were never too far removed from nature to forget that the chief subject of art, in the final sense, is nature." In America, such a society is found in the South, past and present.

In an industrial society—to which the South is being converted, says Davidson—where material progress is the main goal, art is simply one of numerous mass-produced commodities. The industrialist assumes that—by granting the laborer the leisure in which to enjoy art by subsidizing its production, by providing "universal art-education" to the masses, and by distributing it abroad by way of book clubs, libraries, symphonies, and museums—a golden age of the arts will arrive. But, to his dismay, "the arts behave with piggish contrariness. They will not budge, or they run crazily off into briar patches and mud puddles, squealing hideously." What the industrialist fails to realize is that the strenuous, feverish work of the laborer carries over into his leisure life; as a result, he is unable to achieve the calm, harmonious attitude toward work and play required for an appreciation of art. Another false assumption is that everyone can be educated in esthetic appreciation; but, even if it were possible, it would be self-defeating, for the student would be rendered inefficient for his industrial tasks: "The more refined and intelligent he becomes, the more surely will he see in the material world the lack of the image of nobility and beauty that the humanities inculcate in him."

The effect of industrialism on art itself not only brings about a decrease in quality for the sake of quantity but also causes a maladjustment between the artist and society. When he is no longer in accord with society or is driven against it, he may retreat inward, write only of the personal and subjective, and become a romantic: "The poet sings less and less for the crowd in whose experiences he no longer shares intimately. The lonely artist appears, who sings for a narrower and ever diminishing audience; or having in effect no audience, he sings for himself." If the artist refuses to retreat into obscurity, then he must turn to forms of social criticism and protest, which explains the rapid shift in the modern novel "from objective narrative to the problematic, the satirical, the critical." A third alternative is to join the enemy and seek integration with industrial society, by adopting the methods of science, to become an observer, classifier, and recorder; refuse to exercise judgment or principle; and abandon the possibility of tragedy in his work, which is irrelevant "in a world where men behave as their glands make them behave." It is difficult for Davidson to conceive of industrialism as being anything, in the final analysis, but an enemy to art.

His recommendation is that industrialism be repudiated and rejected as the controlling force in modern society. Man should regain a social order which will restore harmony with the artist, and "only in an agrarian society does there remain much hope of a balanced life, where the arts are not luxuries to be purchased but belong as a matter of course in the routine of his living." The South provides the best example of such a society, which Davidson analyzes in cultural and social detail in defense of his belief that the Old South was a well-established, gracious civilization, despite its defects, and was productive of forensics, architecture, folk arts, and literature of a rich and sophisticated quality. The Southern tradition deserves rehabilitation, therefore, for the sake of American culture; and it is still possible in the present if the modern artist—like Ransom, Tate, and Davidson himself—is willing to resist the forces of progressivism by entering the public arena and by taking a stand as a citizen. This is his duty as an artist and a person.[46]

Such a summary as this one, of course, hardly does justice to the burden of Davidson's argument or to the controlled rhetoric of his style; for this essay is a model of clear exposition and verbal grace.

In carrying out their agrarian program, Davidson and the co-authors of *I'll Take My Stand* had plans which extended beyond the publication of a book, although most of them were to remain unrealized. During the year immediately preceding publication, for example, there had been talk on the part of Tate about the formation of a Southern academy composed of "positive reactionaries" drawn from the fields of literature, history, economics, law, and politics, as well as from private citizenry. This academy would have a philosophical constitution, setting forth a complete social, literary, economic, and religious system; and it would spread its ideas through an organized program of publication, with a daily newspaper, a weekly, and a quarterly.[47]

Such an ambitious program obviously would have demanded years of planning, and the book could not wait upon it. When the book created the stir and controversy it did, it was too late to give the academy the attention it would have demanded. Other suggestions which circulated included the founding of a Southern magazine associated with a publishing house and a chain of bookstores for the distribution of publications (suggested by Davidson in 1929), the purchase and publication of a Tennessee county newspaper, the securing of funds for support from a foundation, the formation of a political force by either winning the support of the Democratic party or by uniting with the western agricultural interests, and the writing of a second updated symposium.

Because of this rumination over ways to convey their message to the people, and because of the public controversy the book sparked, the group did organize and carry out a series of public debates on the issue of Agrarianism versus industrialism which generated considerable publicity. The most provocative of the five debates occurred at Richmond, Virginia, under the sponsorship of the Richmond *Times-Dispatch* on the question "Shall the South Be Industrialized?" Stringfellow Barr, who had recently published in the *Virginia Quarterly Review,* which he edited, a sharply critical attack on some of the Agrarians' primary ideas, was confronted by John Crowe Ransom. The moderator was Sherwood Anderson, then owner and publisher of two weekly newspapers in Marion, Virginia, and a writer whose life and work had shown the impress of the opposing currents under debate.

An audience of approximately thirty-five hundred people gathered in the Civic Auditorium on November 14, 1930, to hear the discussion which lasted for two and one-half hours. Ransom's address was carefully organized, sober, and persuasive; but Barr abandoned consecutive argument for a fiery, witty series of abrupt retorts which won the good humor of the audience. Davidson's impression was that "Mr. Barr's pungent sentences won him at times perhaps a bit more applause than Mr. Ransom's very solid and systematic argument got"; and, while it was difficult to declare a winner, he felt encouraged that perhaps the South was "about to renew its old and nearly vanished genius for honest and forthright public argument."[48]

The impact of this initial debate on the news media was so great that Ransom was immediately in demand for subsequent encounters on the same theme, and he argued with *Sewanee Review* editor William S. Knickerbocker in New Orleans on December 15; again with Stringfellow Barr at the University of Chattanooga on January 9, 1931; and at Emory University in Atlanta on February 11 with Georgia industrialist William D. Anderson, who arranged for a mid-debate demonstration by young girls trained in mill schools who sang songs and shouted their love for their paternal capitalist leader. In the last debate held at Columbia, Tennessee, on May 21, 1931, Davidson himself mounted the rostrum in a return engagement with Knickerbocker.

Since Davidson was arguing on home grounds to home folks, he intended to make a speech addressed to the local point of view, he wrote Tate, "making as strong an emotional appeal as I can, because I believe that line—rather than the coolly logical one John [Crowe Ransom] took—is the right one for me. . . . I shall talk about perfectly familiar and immediate things that folks can take to heart."[49] But the prepared text of his remarks, from which he undoubtedly diverged, indicates that he developed a well-organized and clearly reasoned negative statement on the question, "That the future prosperity of the South lies in legally regulated industry." The burden of his argument was one of Ransom's major points in his initial debate: any attempts to instill in industry a sense of moral and social restraint would lead to legal regulation of every aspect of industrial activity. The state would dictate how much could be produced, how much the consumer could purchase, who the employer could hire, how much he could be paid, and ultimately how much he could eat and what clothes he could wear. Such regulation leads finally to state socialism, or, in its extreme character, to Russian communism. In one passage, Davidson hits upon a striking metaphor to explain his attitude:

Those who would argue pro and con on the issue as thus stated are like people who let a dragon into the house and then set about a wild speculation as to whether the dragon should be required to eat in the dining-room or the kitchen, and what his hours of feeding, and his diet should be. And all the time the real argument should be: How shall we get the dragon out of the house in the first place, and back in his den where he will not devour us. I want to get the industrial dragon out of the house, where he never belonged, and back in his proper place, wherever that may be.[50]

In addition to the debates, the individual Agrarians also participated during the following years in various public and institutional conferences where their program and platform could be voiced. But, being primarily men of letters, Davidson, Ransom, Tate, and Warren more often used the printed page as a medium of expression in various periodicals that were not hostile to their attitudes—such as *Virginia Quarterly Review, Hound and Horn, Sewanee Review,* and *Southern Review*—and in other symposia, such as W. T. Couch's *Culture in the South* (1934) and *Who Owns America?,* edited by Herbert Agar and Tate (1936). An especially hospitable outlet was the *American Review* established by Seward Collins in 1933 to offer a traditionalist point of view opposed to the liberal oriented *Nation* and *New Rupublic,* although this connection was later to cause the Agrarians to be labeled Fascists when Collins let his sympathies with Fascism be publicly known.[51] During its four-and-a-half-year duration, the pages of the *American Review* carried more than sixty articles by the Agrarians.

No Agrarian, however, was more active or prolific in his ardent support of the cause than Davidson, who noted in 1932, "We are, after all, writers before everything else—and only secondarily, if at all cavalry commanders, orators, lobbyists, and ward-heelers. We ought to write, then, and keep writing. And we should organize our effort around writing, as we have done in the past, with the sure conviction that if our ideas are right, we shall in the end reach the people who can do the other needful things; and if our ideas are not right, then they deserve to fail."[52] To prove he meant what he said, Davidson published during the decade following the publication of *I'll Take My Stand* over forty essays and one book in further exploration and support of Agrarian principles and on the significance of regionalism in American life. This work he achieved in addition to an impressive number of critical and scholarly essays on literature and regional folkways, a volume of poetry, a textbook anthology of British poetry, and a rhetoric text.

Drawing from his quantity of published essays on regionalism, Davidson assembled and revised in 1937 a selection of the best for *The Attack on Leviathan;* and he prepared, in addition, new material for one-third of the book. Since most of the essays were written over an interval of six years and since Davidson did not thoroughly recast them, the style of the book is not always even and there is a degree of repetition in several pieces—deficiencies which he acknowledged. But, as a compendium of Davidson's thought and as a source of some of his finest prose pieces on the subject of regionalism, the volume is invaluable; it remains, as Richard Weaver noted, "the clearest and most courageous of the Agrarian documents."[53]

Davidson uses interchangeably the terms "sectionalism" and "regionalism" since the latter word has been adopted in place of the former by social scientists who wish to avoid the emotional coloration and contentiousness attached to "sectionalism" in a historical context. As Davidson noted in an earlier essay, "Sectionalism is the political approach to an identical set of facts."[54] For his present purposes, "Politically defined, sectionalism in the United States is the tendency of groups of states, found in physical contiguity and joined by social and economic ties, to think more or less in common and, upon occasion, to act in common."[55]

Regionalism is "the new name for a process of differentiation within geographic limits that is as old as the American republic and perhaps was predestined in the settlement of our continental area. The regionalists are those who wish to see the cultural differences respected, and not thwarted or obliterated. No matter from what field they draw their data—whether historical, scientific, or artistic—the regionalists agree that America, far from being perfectly homogeneous and standardized, is amazingly heterogeneous and diverse."[56] What the regionalists are seeking is "a definition of the terms on which America may have both the diversity and the unity that gives soundness to a tradition. They seek to define the nation in terms of its real and permanent rather than its superficial and temporary qualities. They are learning how to meet the subtlest and most dangerous foe of humanity—the tyranny that wears the mask of humanitarianism and benevolence. They are attacking Leviathan."[57]

The Leviathan he perceives is "the idea of the Great Society, organized under a single, complex, but strong and highly centralized national government, motivated ultimately by men's desire for economic welfare of a specific kind rather than their desire for personal liberty."[58] Leviathan (meaning "that which gathers itself together in folds") is the Hebrew name given to a formidable mythical sea serpent in the Old Testament, and Thomas Hobbes used the word in his treatise *Leviathan, or the Matter, Form and Power of a Commonwealth* (1651) to suggest the civil state, invested with absolute authority over its subjects and institutions, that is necessary to counteract the self-interest he finds responsible for social conflict. Davidson attacks the possibility of such an extreme social contract in this country. The advance of large-scale, industrial economics, which brings conformity and standardization into society, accompanied by a hallowed desire for unity and extreme nationalizing forces, threatens to obliterate the diversity of regionalism. But, Davidson warns, "No Leviathan State can ever abolish sectionalism, unless like Tamerlane it proposes to rule from a pyramid of skulls."[59] While the American government occasionally suggests an awareness of the necessity of a regional approach, as in such federal projects as the Tennessee Valley Authority, its general policy is to deny or conflict with the genuine interests of real social, cultural, and geographic regions.

Davidson rejects the theory of historian Charles A. Beard that economic self-interest was the determining factor in the development of American government. The founding fathers of the nation, Beard believed, operated out of a spirit of economic opportunism instead of religious or democratic convictions. To Davidson, life is not determined by economic forces; rather, life determines economics, which is but an instrument subordinate to other motives. Thus, he preferred the interpretation of Frederick Jackson Turner, who saw, according to Davidson, "that the sections are not vestiges from an older time, archaic and negligible, but have been and still are functions of the national life. They are real entities, not sentimental fiction: they have a place in the making of events, along with the Federal government and the state governments, although their place and power are not yet fully recognized or understood. In Turner's theory, sectionalism is thus organic in the American establishment, but in a creative rather than a negative and destructive sense."[60]

A good deal of *The Attack on Leviathan* is concerned with meticulous verification of the idea that all Americans are not alike and retain local differences according to the region they inhabit, be it the Northeast, South, Southwest, Midwest, Northwest, or Far West. "It still remains a fact that the Puritans settled in New England and men of a different persuasion in Virginia; the Scandinavians went one way, the Scotch-Irish, the Huguenots, the African slave went another way." As a result, "There is no escape from the fact that the American nation is spread over a continental area, and that in the spreading process it has established local concentrations which have geographic bounds."[61]

Perhaps none of Davidson's examinations of the diverse areas is quite as impressive or attractive as his delineation of Brother Jonathan of Vermont and Brother Roderick of Georgia in the essay "Still Rebels, Still Yankees." One thing which accounts for the compelling immediacy of the impression of two quite different states is the fact that Davidson was drawing from his personal experience as a sometime resident of both. The Davidsons were occasional house guests of John Donald Wade in Marshallville, Georgia; and it was, in fact, under the roof of Wade's home that the first essays for *The Attack on Leviathan* were begun. In the summer of 1931, Davidson was invited to teach at the Bread Loaf School of English near Middlebury, Vermont; and he enjoyed the area and people he met there so much that for the remainder of his life he spent most of his summers in Vermont.

Such was the rich quality of his experience in both Vermont and Georgia that Davidson was able to create with seeming ease an evocative description of place and a lively delineation of regional character that have made this essay a frequently reprinted and deserved favorite of prose anthologists since its first appearance in the *American Review* of December, 1933. What it achieves in vivid description and characterization offers effective support as no amount of argumentation could for his central thesis that, while there may be unreconstructed Southerners, "there are unreconstructed Yankees, too, and other unreconstructed Americans of all imaginable sorts, everywhere engaged in preserving their local originality and independence."[62]

Davidson also draws together a formidable body of evidence to substantiate this argument from a variety of areas. The social scientists, such as Rupert Vance and Howard Odum, have proven the significance of regionalism in their sociological analyses because, as soon as they leave an urban setting and approach the countryside, they quickly encounter "the differentiations which are a fundamental part of [the] study of cultures and environments."[63] The growing awareness and utilization of a regional consciousness on the part of American writers, most obviously in the West and South, also suggest the power of its influence. And in folk mythology, in a country which has been unable to agree upon a national heroic type, we "cannot get the intellectual and the emotional element ideally united in the single figure who will stand for what all Americans desire."[64]

Neither Washington, the father of his country, nor Jefferson, the incarnation of the basic democratic ideal, has left us with any feeling or sense of personal presence. While Andrew Jackson, Abraham Lincoln, and Robert E. Lee have left a personal impress as heroic types, they are best understood from regional perspectives: "In the field of myth, . . . the heroes turn out to be sectional, and their sectional particularity is too recognizable for them to be taken over where they are not understood and do not belong."[65] Thus, Davidson's conclusion is that

From many different branches of social study, surveying many different kinds of evidence, one conclusion emerges: sectionalism, or, if one prefers, regionalism, is a persistent and very likely an inherent condition of democratic government in the United States. The only persons who deny this conclusion are those who deny that democratic government can continue. They are extremists who, whether they call themselves idealists or pragmatists, agree in believing that the Leviathan State, in not only a national form but a world form, is necessary to secure to humankind the equal benefits of technological advance, to which they would sacrifice all else.[66]

The biggest task of future generations is to solve the conflict between national and sectional interests, between federalism and regionalism. The ideal condition, he suggests, would be "that the regions should be free to cultivate their own particular genius and to find their happiness, along with their sustenance and security, in the pursuits to which their people are best adapted, the several regions supplementing and aiding each other, in national comity, under a well-balanced economy."[67]

IV   The Poet's Curse

In the decade following the publication of *The Attack on Leviathan,* Davidson continued to develop variations and refinements of his Agrarian and regional ideas, addressing himself to such subjects as the inadequacy of the New Deal for the resolution of Southern problems; the federal subsidization of Northern exploitation of the South and the West through absentee-landlord industry; the idea of vendible, mass-produced culture; and the seeming willful misunderstanding of Agrarianism by critics who castigated *I'll Take My Stand* without bothering to read it—these issues appeared in essays for *Free America,* the *Southern Review, Saturday Review of Literature,* and other publications. But, while the country was paying little heed to his admonitions and appeared bent on establishing certain irreversible trends in its economic and cultural development, Davidson ceased to devote so much of his attention to a defense and explanation of Agrarian principles and expanded his involvement by applying his theories of regionalism to history, literature, and folklore.

Davidson's notable two-volume history of *The Tennessee* in the *Rivers of America* series is an example of his work in history. The study is the rewarding product of several years of extensive research in historical records, geography, and folklore; and, while it was originally planned as a single volume, the editors happily chose to publish it in two volumes instead of attempting to abridge the manuscript. In a style consistently lucid, direct, and smooth—one which Avery Craven characterized as having "something of the lilt of poetry about it and a definite tang of the region of which it tells"[68]—Davidson relates the history of the Tennessee River from the days when the Indians inhabited its shores and made life difficult for the white settlers to the complete reshaping of its course and nature by the momentous forces of technology and engineering controlled by the Tennessee Valley Authority.

As Craven also commented, "He gives the Tennessee a personality and manages to weave about its perverseness, its honest contributions and its occasional waywardness the whole story of the American thrust into this early West and a masterful analysis of Southern ways and values." The narrative is not a superficial account of historical events and a colorless delineation of influential personages. The time Davidson spent traveling and gathering data and firsthand impressions paid off in the authoritative way he could describe the physical qualities of a particular shoal or shore line. But all the data in the world could not have inspired some of the passages; the imagination necessary to re-create with vivid particulars the activities of a place out of the unknowable past is exemplified in this description of Fort Loudoun on the bank of the Little Tennessee on the eve of its tragic role in the French and Indian War:

Fort Loudoun now faced the green world of the Little Tennessee. Twelve cannon overlooked the palisaded bastions. Imposingly they pointed across the savannas and cornfields toward the forest of oak and hickory and poplar and down the clear ripple of the shallow river where pirogues came and went. The British colors rose to the morning gun and sank to the evening gun. Drums sounded the Grenadiers March for the parade, beat the tattoo at dusk, and rolled for reveille while mists marked the curve of the river and many smokes rose from Tuskegee, near by, and from more distant Tomotley. The gates creaked open, the guard changed, red-coated sentries walked post, bayonets fixed. Through the gates flocked Cherokee women, laughing, chattering in their soft forest tongue, carrying baskets of garden truck and wild fruit or of many-colored fish, fresh-caught in the weirs. An old trader passed, his beard thick, his shirt greasy with bear-oil, his Cherokee wife trudging behind him. Through the gate, too, came Old Hop, limping and withered, but stately; or Oconostota, tall and strong, his face pitted from smallpox, a plain-spoken man but every inch the Great Warrior; or the frail, almost delicate figure of the Little Carpenter, clad in a new shirt, frilled and fine, a present from his "brother," the Great Man at Charlestown—the lobes of his ears, distended by silver bangles, drooped to his shoulders, and the shrewd eyes glinted appraisingly below the bare egg-shaped dome of his head where the scalp lock bobbed.[69]

Many of the characters who populate the pages of the volumes are effectively brought to life. The best portraits include those of Sir Alexander Cuming, the flamboyant pioneer confidence man who brashly achieved the incredible mission of gaining submission of the Cherokees to the king of England; John Sevier, known as "Nolichucky Jack," Tennessee's first popular hero and a military genius who earned the love of soldier and citizen alike; or "Old Sawney" Webb, the great

Tennessee schoolmaster who wonderfully combined the frontier tradition with a deep respect for Classical education, as symbolized by his famed erudite cow which would kick if the young scholar standing at its heels failed to conjugate correctly Latin and Greek verbs.

Three of the best portions of the book are Chapter XIX of Volume I, "How It Was in the Old Days," which Avery Craven called "something of a masterpiece," a spirited sketch of life, humor, and folk culture in Tennessee of the 1850's; the first third of volume II, impressive in both style and historical authority, a concise but exciting narrative of the Civil War battles in which the river played a crucial part; and the last chapter of volume II, "Journal of a Voyage from Chattagnooga to Paducah on the Good Steamboat *Gordon C. Greene*," which is a delightful record of Davidson's journey on one of the last few steamboats to travel over two-thirds of the total river length after the Tennessee Valley Authority had wrought its modern miracle of technology.

The clear presence of the author in both art and attitude is one of the books' pervasive qualities, and Davidson's regard for the importance of tradition and regionalism and his attitudes toward the corrupting forces of materialism and technology are evident throughout. Thus, when he describes the commercially calculated treaty in which the Cherokee Indians surrendered property rights to their homeland to the British in return for an insignificant amount of weapons and trinkets, he notes: "The treaty of friendship was in effect a bill of sale. Civilization was beginning its subtle work."[70] Or, when describing one of the newly created Tennessee Valley Authority lakes, he notes: "The river is beautiful here, of course, but a little dull. The kind of made-over beauty that Hollywood prefers."[71]

Some critics have felt that his account of the Tennessee Valley Authority is colored or prejudiced by his opinions; but, knowing undoubtedly that such would be the conclusion of those who had always disagreed with him, Davidson attempted a fair and balanced treatment of both its successes and failures, its regional consciousness and national orientation. He recognized many of the agricultural and social improvements wrought by the Authority; but he is not convinced that these achievements required the dislocation of property owners, the flooding of land, and the drastic changes in nature's face that accompanied the project. Nor is he entirely trustful of the unlimited and independent power granted to this authority by the federal government: "In other days, if you were discontented with a power company, you could appeal to the government. If you were discontented with TVA, to whom did you appeal? TVA was the government. In the Tennessee Valley there was nothing above it."[72]

There is clearly a respect on Davidson's part for the old Tennessee—independent, perverse, dangerous, and sometimes destructive—a respect which cannot be replaced by his awe over its modern counterpart—tamed, gentle, and graced with cold, concrete dams, carefully patterned communities, and scientifically cultivated farm lands. Whether one agrees with Davidson's attitude or not, many have been forced to concede with Gerald W. Johnson that "Such volumes are rarities—so rare that when one appears with the qualities of 'The Tennessee' even a reviewer who disagrees with its tenor in many respects must describe it as distinguished."[73] And a great majority of reviewers agreed when the volumes appeared that *The Tennessee* is history of a distinctive type—authentic, authoritative, and beautifully written.

An excellent cross-section of Davidson's later literary criticism and explorations in regional folklore is contained in his 1957 collection of essays *Still Rebels, Still Yankees*. While the volume includes three essays from *The Attack on Leviathan* and another dated from 1934, the remainder represent work from the 1940's and 1950's; but all are unified by a central concern, which Davidson thus describes: "The general theme that binds the essays—no matter what their specific subjects—is the conflict between tradition and antitradition that characterizes modern society, with tradition viewed as the living continuum that makes society and civilization possible and anti-tradition as the disintegrative principle that destroys society and civilization in the name of science and progress."[74]

The impact of the forces of antitradition are having an effect, Davidson argues, on all manifestations of American culture. Modern poetry, for example, is one gauge of cultural degeneration in that it has a "kind of death-in-life"; existing "only on the printed page, not on the lips of men, [it is] not . . . carried by their voices and therefore almost never carried in their memories, rarely in their hearts."[75] Other signs include the loss of an easy interchange between popular lore and art, both of which, under ideal conditions, pass readily and naturally into the other; the commercial, vulgarizing exploitation of the folk song by the popular singer or hillbilly band; or something as simple as the replacement of the drum major, who served both a utilitarian and ornamental role in the ceremonious marching band, with the frivolous, baton-twirling, bare-fleshed drum majorette, a blatantly sensual perversion of the beautiful and the gallant.

What Davidson finds most disturbing, however, is the triumph in American culture of burlesque over tragedy:

> The tradition of irreverence necessarily arises in a culture where the human impulse for reverence no longer has a worthy object—that is, in a culture where no person, institution, or thing is any longer sacred. In other terms, it is a culture from which the idea of divinity has more or less evaporated and in which, therefore, religion is no longer the arbiter of knowledge. That is what our society has been in process of becoming ever since the sixteenth century—slowly at first, but, since the beginning of the industrial revolution, with the accelerated speed observed and predicted by Henry Adams. We are now predominantly a secular society, ruled by science, theoretical, applied, and "social." In a society ruled by science tragedy becomes an impossible conception, since science must hold that events can be explained, and must essentially be explained, in terms of causes logically describable and logically knowable. The pity and terror that belong to tragedy by the Aristotelian definition are necessarily excluded from the skeptical, inquiring, analytical processes of science. And their exclusion by science means that in the long run they will be excluded from the arts, including the traditional oral arts, or else will be bootlegged in, under some disguise or other.[76]

Davidson's examination of the importance of tradition in literature and in the creative life of the artist is among the most provocative of his essays. His study of Yeats indicates that, while the Irish poet claimed for his art a sense of unity with the tradition and lore of his homeland—as when he said "all art should be a Centaur finding in the popular lore its back and strong legs" tradition was for him in reality merely a subject matter and a part of his literary effects:

> So far as Yeats, therefore, already had, by birthright and direct, naive acquaintance, a hold on popular lore as a subject matter, and went looking for an art to communicate it, he may be said to have built his poetry upon the popular lore, in a way which by implication is desirable. But when he began to think of himself primarily as an artist, and went looking for a subject matter, and decided that he must have a strong back and legs in the popular lore, he did not stem from the popular lore any longer, but merely appropriated it, as he would appropriate any other subject matter, or a metaphor, or a rhyme. The unity of the popular lore and the high art cannot be obtained in this manner.[77]

Writers examined by Davidson who conceive of art as something natural, functional, and properly based upon tradition are Stark Young;

John Gould Fletcher, despite his early allegiance to the primacy of esthetics; and Thomas Hardy, who had more in common with the Realistic, rough-hewn writers of the humor of the Old Southwest than with the Victorian romantic-Realists and French Naturalists, and whose novels may be best understood as constructed after the traditional ballad or oral tale. Both the Yeats and Hardy essays of Davidson have been recognized and reprinted as classic studies of those writers. While all the essays in *Still Rebels, Still Yankees* are variations on previously stated themes and ideas, they offer fresh and important evidence of Davidson's beliefs couched in his usual well-refined style. Together, they provide, as John T. Winterich noted in the *Saturday Review,* "an excellent example of a type of book all too rare in this jet-propelled age: a collection of entertaining literary essays."[78]

Davidson's prose writing did not decrease in his latter years. He turned his hand to revisions of his widely used, well-known composition text *American Composition and Rhetoric;* to scholarly essays and textbooks on education, writing, and rhetoric; to literary and social criticism; to reviews for such publications as the *National Review, Modern Age, Sewanee Review, Georgia Review, New York Times Book Review, Intercollegiate Review,* and the resurrected *Southern Review;* and to valuable autobiographical memoirs of his experiences with the Fugitive and Agrarian groups, two of which—"The Thankless Muse and Her Fugitive Poets" and "Counterattack, 1930-1940: The South Against Leviathan"—were delivered as inaugural lectures at Mercer University in 1957 for the Eugenia Dorothy Blount Lamar Memorial Lectureship and published in *Southern Writers in the Modern World.*

While many of the other eleven authors who joined with Davidson in the Agrarian endeavor of 1930 devoted their labors singly to their own creative work, only Davidson faithfully and consistently developed and defended the principles they then placed their faith in. While his Agrarian endeavors were seldom rewarded by any appreciable effect or influence on American cultural and political life, his voice never faltered nor conceded in the face of sharp criticism, although he was regarded as a romantic, as a reactionary, and as an anachronistic knight, hopelessly fighting a lost cause against the dragons of progress. Recent literary historians and critics of the writings of the Agrarians have pointed out several ways they have been significant in our cultural life: they emphasized the need for maintaining in modern life a sense of the values and traditions that America fell heir to as members of Western European civilization; and they foresaw the development of alarming trends in our industrial society toward conformity, alienation, and dehumanization.

These Agrarian views have been confirmed in the writings of later social analysts, such as David Riesman's *The Lonely Crowd,* W. H. Whyte's *The Organization Man,* Walter Lippmann's *The Public Philosophy,* James P. Warburg's *The West in Crisis,* and Vance Packard's several journalistic exposés. The Agrarians also created a humanistic trend in literature which has rescued it from determinism and amoral scientism, and they tried to restore to man a sense of his own vulnerability and responsibility and thereby re-create in him a sense of tragedy. Without Davidson's persistent and unfailing efforts, these good causes might not have been fought and American literature would have been less rich without his faultless prose.

Undoubtedly at the last he still felt as he did one winter evening only a year after *I'll Take My Stand* appeared, as expressed in a letter to Tate: "I opened our book last night and read many parts again. It is a good thing, that book—a strong, sincere, *right* thing."[79] Writing for the *National Review* in 1960, Davidson could say with some degree of satisfaction: *I'll Take My Stand,* never a best seller, has finally gone into a second edition. As a matter of record I note that the books of those Liberals who assailed us with hootings and catcalls have mostly dropped out of sight."[80] When *Shenandoah* magazine in 1952 submitted to the individual Agrarians a set of questions about their retrospective views of developments since 1930, Davidson reiterated many of his basic beliefs with an even firmer tone of defiance:

The present dominance of industrialism, no matter how formidable, does not prove its inherent goodness or desirability, or predict anything about its permanence. . . . both in 1930 and later, the "Agrarians" condemned the pragmatic approach as one of the most vicious of modern errors. They did not surrender then, and I do not surrender now, to the servile notion that the existence of a powerful "trend" is a mark of its "inevitability." All the works of men result from human choices, human decisions. There is nothing inevitable about them. We are subject to God's will alone, we are not subject to any theory of mechanical determinism originating in "social forces."[81]

In the same symposium, Davidson pointed with the sense of a fulfilled prophet to the verification of the Agrarians' warnings about the course of industrialism:

It has not fulfilled, and cannot fulfill, the buoyant promises made in its name two decades ago by those advocates who, while sneering at the "Agrarians," confidently asserted that industrialism would bring new liberty, more universal happiness, vaster enlightenment, and immense prosperity to the United States at large and to the South in particular. . . . It has provided more and better automobiles, airplanes, refrigerators, and weapons of war—including the atomic bomb. And it has become party to the infliction of war, death, and destruction on an unprecedented scale.[82]

What Davidson was left with was the cold comfort of the "poet's curse," which falls "upon the deaf ears and faceless bodies of modern society," and of which he warned: "However framed, the poet's curse cannot be dismissed as a trifling eccentricity. The historical record will show that it has seldom, if ever, failed to work."[83]

It is difficult to say with any certainty what part Davidson will play in a future literary history of his era. He found himself among friends and colleagues, three of whom—John Crowe Ransom, Allen Tate, and Robert Penn Warren—left the South and attained national and international recognition for their creative achievement. Such a historical fact has made it difficult for Davidson's work to receive a fair and objective assessment as the inevitable comparison of his work with theirs is always misleading. As men of distinctive temperaments and talents, each deserves a separate hearing and this has seldom been accorded Davidson. Yet, as a prose stylist, Davidson has few peers in contemporary American literature. Neither Ransom, Tate, nor Warren has written essays with a precision, a grace, a force, or a conviction to match Davidson's. Because, however, modern society has not been entirely amenable to *what* Davidson had to say, it has little heeded or sought to appreciate *how* he said it. There is every reason to believe, when all is said and done, that Davidson will endure as a prose stylist of the first order in this century.

As a poet, Davidson's work has not been so sharply limited as Ransom's, so intellectually opaque as Tate's, or so undisciplined as Warren's but it is more reasonable to say that his work is distinctive and decidedly different rather than equal or superior to theirs. Actually, it is difficult to compare their achievements because each poet has created from a set of attitudes and poetic principles radically different from those of his fellows. In principle and practice, Davidson wanted to be a poet not of the academy but of the people, which is not to say that he descends to the democratically literal level of a Carl Sandburg. His mature work is closer to that of his Vermont friend and neighbor Robert Frost, in that a minimum of knowledge of poetic technique, and a genuine appreciation of the American language for its potential lyric beauty, enable the reader to yield to the power of his verse.

Like Frost, Davidson turned to the regional experience of his native soil rather than to Europe for his language and subject matter; and, through artistic intensity, he raised this material to a level of universal urgency. Every reading yields a meaning; and, the more often one reads his more successful poems, the fuller the complexity of meaning becomes. And seldom does one find in modern literature, as one does in *The Tall Men,* such a sustained, probing, disturbing poetic analysis of modern man—one that is aware of the influence of his traditional past and fearful of the destruction inherent in the technological path modern society has elected to follow. Because of the totality of Davidson's vision, the seriousness of his intent, and the integrity of his craftsmanship, he merits the attention of posterity.

NOTES AND REFERENCES

Chapter One

1. The historical records for these events, which survived as an oral tradition in Davidson's family, are scanty. They are described in Lewis Preston Summers, *History of Southwest Virginia, 1746-1786, Washington County, 1776-1870* (Richmond, Virginia, 1903; reprinted Baltimore, 1966), p. 380. See also *Goodspeed's History of Tennessee, From the Earliest Time to the Present; Together with an Historical and a Biographical Sketch of Maury, Williamson, Rutherford, Wilson, Bedford and Marshall Counties* (Nashville, 1886), p. 1142, which erroneously locates Andrew Davidson's birthplace as Wales and the origin of the Davidson family as Ireland. The late Mr. Davidson kindly provided the authors with notes on these and the other events described in this chapter. Also helpful is the biographical sketch by Virginia Rock in her dissertation, "The Making and Meaning of *I'll Take My Stand;* A Study in Utopian-Conservatism, 1925-1939," University of Minnesota, 1961, pp. 474-84.

2. *Goodspeed's History of Tennessee,* p. 1142.

3. Davidson, *Southern Writers in the Modern World* (Athens, Georgia, 1958), p. 33. It was with conscious irony, in view of the difference between his economic philosophy and that of Grady, that Davidson added, "And I dutifully exulted in [the name] until, through some uneasiness that I cannot explain, I discarded it in early college days and have since avoided it except for purposes of legal identification."

4. Cited in Louise Davis, "He Clings to Enduring Values," Nashville *Tennessean Magazine,* September 4, 1949, p. 7.

5. Cited in David J. Harkness, "Tennessee in Literature," *The University of Tennessee News Letter,* XXVII (November, 1949), 22.

6. *Ibid.*

7. *Southern Writers in the Modern World,* p. 10.

8. See William O. Batts's brief sketch in his *Private Preparatory Schools for Boys in Tennessee Since 1867* (1957), pp. 29-32.

9. Cited in "Poets of the Spring, Biographical sketches, with selections from their writings," a publicity broadside issued by

Houghton Mifflin upon the occasion of the publication of Davidson's *The Outland Piper* (1924) and other volumes of poetry.

10. For an appreciative essay on William R. ("Sawney") Webb (1842-1926), see Edd Winfield Parks, "Sawney Webb: Tennessee's Schoolmaster," *Segments of Southern Thought* (Athens, Georgia, 1938), pp. 250-72. See also the brief accounts by Edwin Mims and W. R. Webb, Jr., in William O. Batts's *Private Preparatory Schools for Boys in Tennessee Since 1867*, pp. 22-24 and 42-46.

11. *Southern Writers in the Modern World*, p. 9.

12. Louise Cowan, *The Fugitive Group, A Literary History* (Baton Rouge, 1959), pp. 11-12. *Southern Writers in the Modern World*, pp. 10-11.

13. "On Teaching Democracy Through Literature," a paper read at the English teachers section of the conference on "Zeal for American Democracy Day" of the Nashville Public Schools, at Howard School, February 18, 1949, p. 1. Published only in mimeographed form.

14. For a brief history of the school and a sketch by Jesse Wills of its founder, Clarence Blain Wallace, see Batts, *Private Preparatory Schools for Boys in Tennessee Since 1867*, pp. 51-52 and 25-28.

15. "On Teaching Democracy Through Literature," p. 1.

16. The development of Vanderbilt is briefly discussed in Cowan, *The Fugitive Group*, pp. 5-8. For a full history, see Edwin Mims, *History of Vanderbilt University* (Nashville, 1946).

17. *Southern Writers in the Modern World*, pp. 10-11.

18. *Ibid.*, pp. 11-12.

19. Cited in Stanley J. Kunitz and Howard Haycraft, eds., *Twentieth Century Authors* (New York, 1942), p. 350.

20. *Southern Writers in the Modern World*, p. 11.

21. *Ibid.*, p. 12.

22. Cowan, *The Fugitive Group*, p. 22.

23. *Southern Writers in the Modern World*, pp. 13-14.

24. *Ibid.*, p.14.

25. Theresa Sherrer Davidson has had a distinguished career in her own right. After receiving her bachelor and master's degrees in the arts from Oberlin College, she earned a law degree from Vanderbilt in 1922, was admitted to the Tennessee bar, and for awhile served as law librarian at Vanderbilt. Her interest in Roman law led to the earning of a doctoral degree in classics. She was subsequently associate editor and a translator of the Theodosian Code, a part of the larger project for translation of the entire *corpus* of Roman law, under the editorship of Professor Clyde Pharr. She has taught in the Classics department at Vanderbilt and was also a research associate in law for the Brazilian Institute there. Once a student at the Cleveland School of Art, she has always been a talented artist and has illustrated with impressive cuts

three of her husband's works: *The Tennessee* in two volumes, *Still Rebels, Still Yankees,* and *The Long Street.*

26. This account of the history of the 81st Division and the 324th Infantry is based primarily on a chronology, not entirely dependable, published in a souvenir program, *Wildcat National Reunion,* Eighty-First Division, Knoxville, Tennessee, November 8-9-10-11, 1936, with corrections and additional comments provided by Davidson.

27. The three friends were Stephen F. Shackelford of Charleston, South Carolina; S. Toof Brown of Memphis, Tennessee; and John F. Stevens of Greensboro, North Carolina. Mr. Shackelford died in 1963. In response to inquiries by the authors, the other two friends indicate they have either lost or misplaced their copies of the poems during moves over the years, but Davidson provided the authors with manuscript copies.

28. "The Roman Road," *The Long Street* (Nashville, 1961), p. 80.

29. Letter to the authors from S. Toof Brown, dated August 4, 1964.

30. *The Tall Men* (Boston, 1927), pp. 66-67.

Chapter Two

1. Davidson, *Southern Writers in the Modern World* (Athens, Georgia, 1958), p. 11.

2. Conversation with Davidson, June 2, 1966.

3. *Ibid.*

4. Four sections of freshman composition for two hours each; during a third hour, all freshman sections met in a combined group to hear Mims's lectures on literature.

5. *Southern Writers in the Modern World,* p. 21.

6. In November, 1921, when Tate attended his first meeting, the group was composed of Walter Clyde Curry, Donald Davidson, James M. Frank, Sidney Mttron Hirsch, Stanley Johnson, John Crowe Ransom, and Alec. B. Stevenson. Merrill Moore joined in the following spring, soon after the first issue of *The Fugitive* was published in April, 1922. William Yandell Elliott and William Frierson were members *in absentia;* both being in England as Rhodes scholars, they could not attend meetings except during vacations. Jesse and Ridley Wills became members later in 1922, Robert Penn Warren in 1924, and Laura Riding in 1925. (In the margin of his copy of Allen Tate's "The Fugitive 1922-25: A Personal Recollection Twenty Years After," *Princeton University Library Chronicle,* III April, 1942, pp. 75-84, Davidson notes: "Laura Riding Gottschalk was never a *real* member—only 'honorary,' because she won a Fugitive poetry prize and soon after paid the Fugitives a short visit. In the effusion of the moment 'Dr. Hirsch,'

speaking *ex cathedra,* said we must make Laura a member. Alas, we did! That was the only meeting Laura attended.")

7. Tate, "The Fugitive 1922-25," p. 76.

8. *Ibid.,* p. 77.

9. Louise Cowan, *The Fugitive Group* (Baton Rouge, 1959), pp. 39-40.

10. *Southern Writers in the Modern World,* p. 3.

11. *Ibid.,* p. 8.

12. Tate gives Hirsch credit for naming *The Fugitive* ("The Fugitive, 1922-25," p. 78), but Davidson notes in the margin of his copy of Tate's essay: "Not exactly right. Alec Stevenson gave the name (or so I recollect). But 'Fugitive' was a term often used by Hirsch in a symbolic mystical sense."

13. Cowan, *The Fugitive Group,* p. 44.

14. Tate, "The Fugitive 1922-25," p. 79.

15. Notation in the margin of Davidson's copy of Tate's essay "The Fugitive 1922-25."

16. The poems receiving more votes than "The Dragon Book" were Ransom's "L'Egoist" and Stanley Johnson's "Sermons."

17. During the three years that *The Fugitive* was published, his salary was not far above the fourteen hundred dollars for which he returned to Vanderbilt.

18. Letter to Tate, dated January 12, 1923.

19. Letter to Tate, dated January 23, 1923.

20. Randall Stewart, "Donald Davidson," *South: Modern Southern Literature in Its Cultural Setting,* Louis D. Rubin, Jr., and Robert D. Jacobs, eds. (Garden City, New York, 1961), p. 253.

21. Tate, "The Fugitive 1922-25," p. 79.

22. "Foreword," *The Fugitive,* I (April, 1922), p. 1.

23. *Southern Writers in the Modern World,* p. 5.

24. Undated letter to Laura Riding written in 1924.

25. Davidson wrote Tate on July 25, 1922: "I am quite sure that you are better posted on the subject matter and techniques that I have recently assayed than any others of our Fugitive Group. Likewise you have given me keener and more helpful criticisms than anybody who ever read my poems, and your ideas and theories have wonderfully quickened and leavened my stodgy mind." He returned to the subject of Tate's criticism, after many comments in between, more than thirty years later: "The most helpful criticism I ever received—and the sternest—was from Allen Tate, in the marginal notations on manuscripts that I sent him and in the very frank letters that always came with the return of a manuscript" (*Southern Writers in the Modern World,* p. 22). For a discussion of Tate's influence on the composition of Davidson's "Lee in the Mountains," see Thomas Daniel Young and M. Thomas

Inge, *Donald Davidson: An Essay and a Bibliography* (Nashville, 1965), pp. 3-44.

26. *Southern Writers in the Modern World*, pp. 22-23.

27. *Ibid.*, p. 23.

28. *Ibid.*, p. 28.

29. *Ibid.*

30. Davidson, *The Spyglass: Views and Reviews, 1924-1930,* John Tyree Fain, ed. (Nashville, 1963), p.v.

31. Cowan, *The Fugitive Group*, p. xv.

32. The quotation is from an undated letter, written in late 1924, from Davidson to Laura Riding Gottschalk. The magazines in which Davidson's poems had appeared, in addition to *The Fugitive,* include *Palms, The Measure, Folio, The Reviewer, The Double Dealer,* and *The Sewanee Review.*

33. Within the next two or three years Davidson's poems were printed in several more anthologies, including Edwin Markham's *The Book of Poetry* (1926), L. A. G. Strong's *The Best Poems of 1926,* Jessie B. Rittenhouse's *The Third Book of Modern Verse* (1926), and Addison Hibbard's *The Lyric South* (1928). *Fugitives: An Anthology of Verse* also appeared in 1928.

34. *The Nation,* CXVIII (April 2, 1924), 376.

35. Boston *Transcript,* May 10, 1924.

36. *Poetry,* XXIV (September, 1924), 344.

37. Philadelphia *Public Ledger,* March 23, 1924.

38. Lexington (Kentucky) *Herald,* March 23, 1924.

39. *Bookman,* LIX (May, 1924), 346-48.

40. *Outlook,* CXXXVI (April, 1924), 640-50.

41. *Double Dealer,* VI (August-September, 1924), 209-10.

42. Letter from Tate to Davidson, dated October 5, 1924.

43. *Southern Writers in the Modern World*, p. 22.

44. Letter to Tate, dated January 12, 1923. "The Dragon Book" and "The Valley of the Dragon" were not included in *An Outland Piper.*

45. The poems included in *An Outland Piper* (Boston, 1924) are divided into four groups. Although the different sections are unnamed, each is headed by a Roman numeral which is followed by the title of the first poem appearing in that section. Our discussion of the individual poems in the collection follows this plan of organization.

46. In *Poems 1922-1961,* Davidson changes the title to "The Outland Piper." The version printed in *An Outland Piper* and *Poems* omits two stanzas which were included when the poem first appeared in *The Fugitive* (April, 1922). These two stanzas, one of which stood at the beginning and the other at the end, provided a kind of frame for the poem.

> Old Man, what are you looking for?
> Why do you tremble so, at the window peering in?
> —A Brother of mine! that's what I'm looking for!
> Someone I sought and lost of noble kin.
>
> . . . . .
>
> Old man, is it songs you are looking for?
> Music lost in the leaf that the year has shed?
> —A Brother of mine! that's what I'm looking for!
> The sight of a kinsman's face before I am dead.

47. John L. Stewart, *The Burden of Time: The Fugitives and Agrarians* (Princeton, 1965), p. 54. Stewart's reading of all of Davidson's poetry is startingly inexact and his treatment of Davidson is highly opionionated.

49. Twelve Southerners, *I'll Take My Stand,* Harper Torchbook Edition (New York, 1962), p. 51. (The pagination of this reprint is the same as that of the 1930 edition.)

50. *Ibid.,* p. 36.

51. Davidson, "Poetry as Tradition," *Still Rebels, Still Yankees,* p. 21. This essay was first given as an address before the Alpha of Tennessee Chapter of Phi Beta Kappa in 1956.

52. *Ibid,.* p. 20.

53. *Ibid,.* p. 22.

54. *Southern Writers in the Modern World,* p. 22.

55. The best poems in this section were not published in *The Fugitive,* but in *The Double Dealer;* "Corymba" and "Dryad" appearing in October, 1922; "Naiad" in November, 1922; and "Twilight Excursion" in January, 1923. "Avalon" was first printed, along with Ransom's "Armageddon" and William Alexander Percy's "A Fragment," in the 1923 *Yearbook of the Poetry Society of South Carolina.*

56. Letter from Tate to Davidson, dated August 13, 1922.

57. Letter to Tate, dated July 8, 1922.

58. *Southern Writers in the Modern World,* p. 28.

59. This manuscript showing Tate's comments is among Davidson's private papers on deposit in the Joint University Libraries, Nashville, Tennessee. It is reproduced, however, in Cowan, *The Fugitive Group,* facing p. 168.

60. Apparently dissatisfied with the last two lines of the poem, in his personal copy of *An Outland Piper* Davidson revised them as follows: "And lost? Rags cast-off by the age/ And left to mask the sterile pool."

61. Letter to Tate, dated July 25, 1922. That Davidson is somewhat concerned about the subject matter of these poems is suggested by a half-facetious remark included in a letter written to Tate on August 23,

1922: "My friends would think I'm a pornographic wretch if 'Corymba,' 'Dryad,' and 'Naiad' were published."

62. The other four are "A Dead Romanticist," "Redivivus," "Old Harp," and "The Demon Brother" ("An Outland Piper").

63. Letter to Tate, dated July 15, 1922.

Chapter Three

1. Davidson, *Southern Writers in the Modern World* (Athens, Georgia, 1958), p. 3.

2. *The Fugitive,* IV (December, 1925), 125.

3. Letter to Tate, dated March 15, 1926.

4. Letter to Tate, dated January 28, 1928.

5. Davidson was writing the long poem, published in 1927 as *The Tall Men;* Tate, among others, his "Ode to the Confederate Dead."

6. Louise Cowan, *The Fugitive Group* (Baton Rouge, 1959), p. 102.

7. Letter to John Hall Wheelock, dated February 4, 1949.

8. *Ibid.*

9. In its first published version *The Tall Men* was composed of ten separate poems, one of which ("Resurrection") was dropped after the first issue (Boston: Houghton Mifflin Company, 1927).

10. In a letter to the authors (August 24, 1964) Davidson writes: "Ransom, later, spoke of industrialism as initiating 'the infinite series.' "

11. Louise Cowan, "Donald Davidson: "The Long Street," *Reality and Myth,* W. E. Walker and R. L. Welker, eds. (Nashville, 1964), p. 116.

12. In addition to the Prologue and the title poem, *The Tall Men* contains "The Sod of Battle Fields," "Geography of the Brain," "The Faring," "Conversation in a Bedroom," "The Breaking Mould," "Epithalamion," and "Fire on Belmont Street."

13. *The Southern Writer in the Modern World,* p. 42.

14. Letter to R. N. Linscott dated April 9, 1927.

15. In the publicity material sent to John Hall Wheelock, February 4, 1949, Davidson wrote about this incident: "A great many of the incidental details and small episodes embodied in *The Tall Men* came to me from my father. Other material, especially in the section called 'The Sod of Battle-fields,' came to me, in childhood, from my grandmother, Rebecca Patton Wells. She, as a young woman, lived through and witnessed certain events that I relate, including the capture and wanton killing of the three young Confederate soldiers. This particular happening is still remembered, as an event of local history, at Chapel Hill. The historians, busy with their explanations of large issues, do not seem to realize such an affair was a common, not an uncommon, event or that such things are remembered still."

16. He wrote Wheelock on February 4, 1949: "But the material in *The Tall Men* is of course a blend of what I learned from my folks and other folks, by word of mouth; what I got from regular history books; and what I myself experienced."

17. All of these places Davidson, of course, knew well, not only from books but from personal experiences. White attending Branham and Hughes School at Spring Hill, Tennessee, the railroad station he used was Ewell's Station. Franklin is only twenty miles from Nashville, where Davidson lived for most of his adult life.

18. Letter to Linscott, dated April 9, 1927.

19. *Ibid.*

20. John Gould Fletcher, *Nation,* CXXVI (January 18, 1928), 71.

21. Davidson says the 81st Division, "the first to wear a shoulder insignia, used a 'Wildcat' as its totem." Letter from Davidson to authors, August 24, 1964.

22. "All American soldiers who passed through England in the great troop movement of the summer of 1918 received an official letter of 'welcome' (a form letter, of course, but a very handsome one) signed by King George V." *Ibid.*

23. " 'The Faring' may well reflect my dissatisfaction, if not my disgust," Davidson has written, "with the 'war novels' that Dos Passos, Hemingway and company wrote during the twenties. I have never known anyone who served with a combat division who thought highly of Dos Passos' *Three Soldiers* or of Hemingway's *A Farewell to Arms.* These books, to the men in the fighting lines, reflected the 'soft' outlook of the men in the Service of Supply." *Ibid.* See also Davidson's review of *A Farewell to Arms,* Nashville *Tennessean,* November 3, 1929.

24. In 1919, in Cleveland, Ohio, Davidson had a totally unsatisfactory experience with a veterans' employment agency.

25. Randall Stewart, "Donald Davidson," *South: Modern Southern Literature in its Cultural Setting,* Louis D. Rubin, Jr., and Robert D. Jacobs, eds. (Garden City, 1961), p. 256.

26. John Crowe Ransom, review of *The Tall Men,* Nashville *Tennessean,* October 2, 1927.

27. Davidson says this episode, like the World War I experiences of McCrory in "The Faring" and unlike most of the incidents of "The Tall Men" and "The Sod of Battle-fields," is entirely imaginary. Interview, June 7, 1964.

28. The poem was first published in the *Yearbook of the Poetry Society of South Carolina* (Spring, 1926).

29. *Southern Writers in the Modern World,* p. 41.

30. Cowan, "Donald Davidson, The 'Long Street,' "p. 116.

31. Letter to R. N. Linscott of Houghton Mifflin, dated April 9, 1927.

32. Davidson, "A Mirror for Artists," *I'll Take My Stand,* Harper Torchbook Edition (New York, 1962), p. 44.

Chapter Four

1. Andrew Nelson Lytle, "The Son of Man: He Will Prevail," *Sewanee Review,* LXIII (1955), 114-37.

2. *Ibid.*

3. "Introduction," Twelve Southerners, *I'll Take My Stand,* Harper Torchbook Edition (New York, 1962), p. xxiv.

4. *Ibid.,* p. xxv.

5. Letter to John Hall Wheelock, dated February 4, 1949.

6. "Introduction," *I'll Take My Stand,* p. xxiv.

7. Psalm 121.

8. First published in the *American Review* for May, 1934, this poem has been reprinted in more than a dozen textbooks, anthologies, and collections of modern verse, including the three editions of *Understanding Poetry* by Cleanth Brooks, Jr., and Robert Penn Warren. See Thomas Daniel Young and M. Thomas Inge, *Donald Davidson: An Essay and a Bibliography* (Nashville, 1965), p. 73.

9. Louise Cowan, "Donald Davidson: 'The Long Street,' " *Reality and Myth,* William E. Walker and Robert L. Welker, eds. (Nashville, 1964), p. 112.

10. Lawrence E. Bowling, "An Analysis of Davidson's 'Lee in the Mountains,' " *Georgia Review,* VI (Spring, 1952), 69.

11. Letter from Tate to Davidson, dated January 19, 1934.

12. Davidson, *Southern Writers in the Modern World* (Athens, Georgia, 1958), p. 60.

13. *Ibid.,* p. 60.

14. *Ibid.,* pp. 60-61.

15. In "An Analysis of Donald Davidson's 'Lee in the Mountains' " Professor Lawrence E. Bowling offers a detailed discussion of the poem's five-part structure and of Davidson's use of historical details in the composition of the poem. For a discussion of the procedure Davidson followed in writing the poem and of his reactions to Tate's comments on a draft of the poem before it was published, see Young and Inge, *Donald Davidson: An Essay and a Bibliography,* pp. 3-44.

16. Letter from Tate to Davidson, dated January 19, 1934.

17. *Ibid.*

18. *Ibid.*

19. Bowling, "An Analysis of Donald Davidson's 'Lee in the Mountains,' " p. 73.

20. That Lee seriously considered the possibility of taking his army to the mountains and continuing the war from there is indicated by a

statement made by Jefferson Davis at a memorial service for Gen. Lee, November 3, 1870, and reported in the Richmond *Dispatch,* November 4, 1870: "When in the last campaign he was beleaguered at Petersburg, and painfully aware of the straits to which we were reduced, he said, 'With my army in the mountains of Virginia I could carry on this war for twenty years longer.' . . . In surrender he anticipated conditions that have not been fulfilled." (Quoted by Hudson Strode in *Jefferson Davis, Tragic Hero: The Last Twenty-Five Years, 1864-1889* [New York, 1964], p. 370.)

21. "The Ninth Part of Speech" is subtitled " A Verse Letter: To Louis Zahner." Although he was the Head of the English Department at Groton, Louis Zahner taught during the summers at Bread Loaf. One afternoon Davidson and Mrs. Davidson went to visit their neighbor, who was living in a building that had once been a schoolhouse, but discovered that Zahner was not at home. The poem comes from this incident.

22. Davidson, *Still Rebels, Still Yankees and Other Essays* (Baton Rouge, 1957), pp. 25-26.

23. *I'll Take My Stand,* p. 44.

24. *Still Rebels, Still Yankees,* p. 27.

25. Quoted by Curtis Bradford, "Yeat's Byzantium Poems: A Study of Their Development," *Yeats: A Collection of Critical Essays,* John Unterecker, ed. (Englewood Cliffs, New Jersey, 1963), p. 96.

26. *Still Rebels, Still Yankees,* p. 171.

27. *I'll Take My Stand,* p. 51.

Chapter Five

1. Letter to Tate, dated January 28, 1934.

2. Louis D. Rubin, Jr., in his review of *Still Rebels, Still Yankees* for the Baltimore *Sun,* March 21, 1957.

3. Gerald W. Johnson in his review of the second volume of *The Tennessee* for the New York *Herald Tribune Weekly Book Review,* January 25, 1948.

4. Essay: III (June, 1924), 66-68; reviews: IV (June, 1925), 61-62; IV (June, 1925), 62-63; IV (September, 1925), 94-95; IV (December, 1925), 126-28.

5. Davidson, "Joseph Conrad's Directed Indirections," *Sewanee Review,* XXXIII (April, 1925), 177.

6. Davidson, "Essays on Conrad's 'Suspense,' IV" *Saturday Review of Literature,* II (November 21, 1925), 315.

7. Letter to Tate, dated August 22, 1923. Also mentioned in a letter of August 30, 1923.

8. For a complete list on contributors see the appendix to Donald Davidson, *The Spyglass, Views and Reviews, 1924-1930,* selected and edited by John Tyree Fain (Nashville, 1963), pp. 257-59. For an excellent account of Davidson's years as editor of the *Tennessean* book page, see Fain's introduction, pp. v-xviii.

9. Letter to Tate, dated March 21, 1928.

10. Ernest Hartsock, "Roses in the Desert," *Sewanee Review,* XXXVII (July, 1925), 333.

11. Howard Mumford Jones, "Is There a Southern Renaissance?," *Virginia Quarterly Review,* VI (April, 1930), 185.

12. For a check-list of the books reviewed, see "Nashville Tennessean Book Page Reviews," in Thomas Daniel Young and M. Thomas Inge, *Donald Davidson: An Essay and a Bibliography* (Nashville, 1965), 94-107. A selection of the best reviews and essays are reprinted in *The Spyglass.*

13. See especially his reviews of Hemingway in *The Spyglass,* pp. 77-79, 88-92, which are much in accord with some recent reevaluations of Hemingway's work, and his perceptive Faulkner reviews, reprinted with an introduction in M. Thomas Inge, "Donald Davidson on Faulkner: An Early Recognition," *Georgia Review,* XX (Winter, 1966), 454-62. For a discussion of Davidson's contributions to Faulkner's reputation, see O. B. Emerson, "Prophet Next Door," *Reality and Myth,* W. E. Walker and R. L. Welker, eds. (Nashville, 1964), pp. 237-74.

14. *The Spyglass,* pp. 15-16.

15. *Ibid.,* pp. 34, 41-42.

16. Davidson, "The Artist as Southerner," *Saturday Review of Literature,* II (May 15, 1926), 781-83.

17. *The Spyglass,* pp. 3-4.

18. *Ibid.,* p. 134.

19. *Ibid.,* p. 231.

20. *Ibid.,* p. 193.

21. *Ibid.,* p. 228.

22. *Ibid.,* p. 202.

23. *Ibid.,* p. 88.

24. Letter to Tate, dated December 29, 1929.

25. The following passage is representative of the kind of confusion in the popular and scholarly mind about the relation of the two groups: "Take away the demagogs, bigotries, poverties, and sometimes deprivations, or, rather, forget about that side of Southern agriculture and remember the ideal and approachable way of which the Nashville 'Fugitives' wrote in their immortal volume ('I'll Take My Stand') – and you have the hope and need of America's years to come." John Temple Graves, *The Fighting South* (New York, 1943), p. 176.

26. Louise Cowan, *The Fugitive Group* (Baton Rouge, 1959), p. xvi. Mrs. Cowan lists as Agrarians: Ransom, Davidson, Tate, Warren,

Andrew Lytle, Stark Young, John Gould Fletcher, Frank Lawrence Owsley, Lyle Lanier, Henry Clarence Nixon, John Donald Wade, and Henry Blue Kline.

27. Louise Cowan, "The Fugitive Poets in Relation to the South," *Shenandoah*, VI (Summer, 1955), 9.

28. Richard Weaver, "Agrarianism in Exile," *Sewanee Review*, LVIII (October, 1950), 589-90.

29. Rob Roy Purdy, ed., *Fugitives' Reunion, Conversations at Vanderbilt May 3-5, 1956* (Nashville, 1959), p. 181.

30. *Ibid.*, p. 218.

31. Letter to Tate, dated February 25, 1930.

32. Twelve Southerners, *I'll Take My Stand*, Harper Torchbook Edition (New York, 1962), p. 42.

33. Robert Shafer, "Humanism and Impudence," *Bookman*, LXX (January, 1930), 489-98. For an account of the controversy in fuller detail, see Virginia Rock's unpublished dissertation, "The Making and Meaning of *I'll Take My Stand:* A Study in Utopian Conservatism, 1925-1939," University of Minnesota, 1961, pp. 272-76.

34. For a thorough comparison of Jefferson and the Agrarians, see Patrick F. Quinn, "Agrarianism and the Jeffersonian Philosophy," *Review of Politics*, II (January, 1940), 87-104.

35. The Calhoun relationship has been questioned by Ann Ward Amacher, in "Myths and Consequences, Calhoun and Some Nashville Agrarians," *South Atlantic Quarterly*, LIX (1960), 251-64.

36. *Fugitives' Reunion*, p. 199.

37. Davidson, *Southern Writers in the Modern World* (Athens, Georgia, 1958), p. 40.

38. Cowan, "The Fugitive Poets in Relation to the South," pp. 6-7.

39. When Allen Tate wrote Davidson from Paris in February, 1929, of his growing interest in Catholicism, Davidson responded that he too had inclinations toward Catholicism or High Church Episcopalianism, although he preferred to be attached to no church at all. Were it not for the clergy and the priesthood, he noted, he might have joined some religious organization; but religious matters seemed to bother him less than anything else. He did, nevertheless, agree that religion was important to the fully integrated Agrarian society. Letter to Tate, July 29, 1929.

40. "The Artist as Southerner," *Saturday Review of Literature*, II (May 15, 1926), p. 783.

41. Davidson, "First Fruits of Dayton," *Forum*, LXXIX (June, 1928), 898, 899, 901, 902-3, 901, and 906.

42. Virginia Rock establishes the year as 1926 and provides a thorough account of the project's evolution in her dissertation, "The Making and Meaning of *I'll Take My Stand*," pp. 222-67. Much of the

content of this chapter is heavily indebted to Virginia Rock's scholarly and thorough spade work on the Agrarians and *I'll Take My Stand.*

43. See Rock, p. 242, note 2.

44. "Contributors and Subjects," accompanying a letter to Davidson, dated August 10, 1929.

45. *I'll Take My Stand,* p. xxv.

46. *Ibid.,* pp. 29, 34, 44, 45, 46, 51-52.

47. Letter to Davidson, dated August 10, 1929.

48. Davidson, "Whither Dixie—Mr. Barr and Mr. Ransom in the Great Debate at Richmond," Chattanooga *News,* XLIII (November 22, 1930), 25.

49. Letter to Tate, dated April 14, 1931.

50. From the unpublished typescript of Davidson's notes in his personal papers.

51. For an excellent account and refutation of the fascism charge, see Rock, "The Making and Meaning of *I'll Take My Stand,*" pp. 401-412. See also Albert E. Stone, Jr., "Seward Collins and the *American Review:* Experiment in Pro-Fascism, 1933-1937," *American Quarterly,* XII (Spring, 1960), 4-19.

52. Letter to Tate, dated October 29, 1932.

52. Richard Weaver, "Agrarianism in Exile," p. 596.

54. Davidson, "Where Regionalism and Sectionalism Meet," *Social Forces,* XIII (October, 1934), 25.

55. Davidson, *The Attack on Leviathan, Regionalism and Nationalism in the United States* (Chapel Hill, 1938), p. 23.

56. *Ibid.,* p. 243.

57. *Ibid.,* p. 12.

58. *Ibid.,* p. 33.

59. *Ibid.,* p. 106.

60. *Ibid.,* p. 9.

61. *Ibid.,* p. 5.

62. *The Attack on Leviathan,* p. 131.

63. *Ibid.,* p. 40. See the entire essay, "Social Science Discovers Regionalism," pp. 39-64.

64. *Ibid.,* p. 218.

65. *Ibid.,* p. 225.

66. *Ibid.,* p. 102.

67. *Ibid.,* p. 110.

68. Avery Craven, Review of *The Tennessee,* Vol. I, New York *Herald Tribune Weekly Book Review,* October 27, 1946, p. 4.

69. Davidson, *The Tennessee, I: The Old River, Frontier to Secession* (New York, 1946), pp. 111-13.

70. *Ibid.,* p. 91.

71. Davidson, *The Tennessee, II: The New River, Civil War to TVA* (New York, 1948), p. 348.

72. *Ibid.*, p. 333.

73. Said with regard to volume II in a review by Gerald W. Johnson, New York *Herald Tribune Weekly Book Review*, January 25, 1948.

74. From a quotation on the book jacket for Davidson's *Still Rebels, Still Yankees and Other Essays* (Baton Rouge, 1957).

75. *Ibid.*, p. 20.

76. *Ibid.*, pp. 124-25.

77. *Ibid.*, p. 28.

78. John T. Winterich, Review of *Still Rebels, Still Yankees, Saturday Review*, XL (May 4, 1957), 50.

79. Letter to Tate, dated December 19, 1931.

80. Davidson, "The New South and the Conservative Tradition," *National Review*, IX (September 10, 1960), 145.

81. "A Symposium: The Agrarians Today," *Shenandoah*, III (Summer, 1952), 16-17.

82. *Ibid.*, p. 17.

83. *Still Rebels, Still Yankees*, p. 5.

SELECTED BIBLIOGRAPHY

For an exhaustive bibliography of Davidson's books, pamphlets, poems, essays, and book reviews, and an annotated list of biographical and critical material, through 1964, the reader is referred to the authors' *Donald Davidson: An Essay and a Bibliography* (Nashville: Vanderbilt University Press, 1965). The present selective list is limited to the more significant works, supplemented by items that have appeared since 1964.

PRIMARY SOURCES

1. BOOKS

An Outland Piper. (Poems.) Boston and New York: Houghton Mifflin Company, 1924.

The Tall Men. (Poems.) Boston and New York: Houghton Mifflin Company, 1927.

British Poetry of the Eighteen-Nineties. (Anthology.) Garden City, New York: Doubleday, Doran & Company, 1937.

The Attack on Leviathan: Regionalism and Nationalism in the United States. (Essays.) Chapel Hill: University of North Carolina Press, 1938.

Lee in the Mountains and Other Poems, Including The Tall Men. (Poems.) Boston and New York: Houghton Mifflin Company, 1938. Reissued by Charles Scribner's Sons, 1949.

American Composition and Rhetoric. (Textbook.) New York: Charles Scribner's Sons, 1939. Reissues and revisions: 1943, 1947, 1953, 1959, 1964, 1968.

Readings for Composition from Prose Models. (Textbook.) Edited with Sidney Erwin Glenn. New York: Charles Scribner's Sons, 1942. Revised 1957.

The Tennessee. 2 volumes. The Rivers of America Series. New York and Toronto: Rinehart & Company, 1946 and 1948.

Twenty Lessons in Reading and Writing Prose. (Textbook.) New York: Charles Scribner's Sons, 1955.

Still Rebels, Still Yankees. (Essays.) Baton Rouge: Louisiana State University Press, 1957.

Southern Writers in the Modern World. Lamar Memorial Lectures. Athens: University of Georgia Press, 1958.

The Long Street: Poems. Nashville: Vanderbilt University Press, 1961.

The Spyglass: Views and Reviews, 1924-1930. (Book reviews and essays.) Selected and edited by John Tyree Fain. Nashville: Vanderbilt University Press, 1963.

Poems: 1922-1961. Minneapolis: University of Minnesota Press, 1966.

Selected Essays and Other Writings of John Donald Wade. Edited with an Introduction by Donald Davidson. Athens: University of Georgia Press, 1966.

Voltmeier, or The Mountain Men. The Writings of William Gilmore Simms. Vol. I. Introduction and Explanatory Notes by Donald Davidson and Mary C. Simms Oliphant. Columbia: University of South Carolina Press, 1969.

2. ESSAYS AND ARTICLES (uncollected)

"A Mirror for Artists." Twelve Southerners. *I'll Take My Stand.* New York: Harper and Brothers Publishers, 1930. Pp. 28-60. Reissued with an Introduction by Louis D. Rubin, Jr. and Biographical Sketches by Virginia Rock, Harper Torchbooks, 1962.

"Agrarianism and Politics." *Review of Politics,* I (April, 1939), 114-25.

"Artist as Southerner." *Saturday Review of Literature,* II (May 15, 1926), 781-83.

"Decorum in the Novel." *Modern Age,* IX Winter, 1964-65), 34-48.

"First Fruits of Dayton, the Intellectual Evolution in Dixie." *Forum,* LXXIX (June, 1928), 896-907.

" 'I'll Take My Stand': A History." *American Review,* V (Summer, 1935), 301-21.

"Introduction." *The Fugitive: April, 1922 to December, 1925.* Gloucester, Massachusetts: Peter Smith, 1967. Pp. i-vii.

"Joseph Conrad's Directed Indirections." *Sewanee Review,* XXXIII (April, 1925), 163-77.

"Political Regionalism and Administrative Regionalism." *Annals of the American Academy of Political and Social Science,* CCVII (January, 1940), 138-43.

"Preface to Decision." *Sewanee Review,* LIII (Summer, 1945), 394-412.

"The Meaning of War: A Note on Allen Tate's 'To the Lacedemonians.' " *Southern Review,* I (July, 1965), 720-30.

"The 'Mystery' of the Agrarians: Facts and Illusions About Some Southern Writers." *Saturday Review of Literature,* XXVI (January 23, 1943), 6-7.

"The New South and the Conservative Tradition." *National Review,* IX (September 10, 1960), 141-46.

"The Political Economy of Regionalism." *American Review VI (February, 1936), 410-34.*

"The Trend of Literature: A Partisan View." W. T. Couch, ed. *Culture in the South.* Chapel Hill: University of North Carolina Press, 1935. Pp. 183-210.

"The Vision of Richard Weaver: A Foreword." Richard M. Weaver. *The Southern Tradition at Bay.* Edited by George Core and M. E. Bradford. New Rochelle, N. Y.:Arlington House, 1968. Pp. 13-25.

"Where Regionalism and Sectionalism Meet." *Social Forces,* XIII (October, 1934), 23-31.

"White Spirituals: The Choral Music of the South." *American Scholar,* IV (Autumn, 1935), 460-73.

"Whither Dixie? Mr. Barr and Mr. Ransom in the Great Debate at Richmond." Chattanooga *News,* November 22, 1930, p. 25.

SECONDARY SOURCES

BEATTY, RICHMOND CROOM. "Donald Davidson as Fugitive-Agrarian." *Hopkins Review,* V (Winter, 1952), 12—27. Reprinted in Louis D. Rubin, Jr., and Robert D. Jacobs, eds. *Southern Renascence.* Baltimore: Johns Hopkins Press, 1953. Summarizes the central ideas of Davidson's prose and poetry.

BOWLING, LAWRENCE E. "An Analysis of Davidson's 'Lee in the Mountains.'" *Georgia Review,* VI (Spring, 1952), 69—88. Thorough historical explication of the poem.

BRADBURY, JOHN M. *The Fugitives: A Critical Account.* Chapel Hill: University of North Carolina Press, 1958. Unsympathetic, imperceptive readings of Davidson as a "bitterly disillusioned romantic."

BRADFORD, M. E. "A Comment on the Poetry of Davidson." *Mississippi Quarterly,* XIX (Winter, 1965-66), 41—43. On the use of two Nashville scenes in "On a Replica of the Parthenon," and "Twilight on Union Street."

————. "Donald Davidson: 1893—1968." *Southern Review,* IV (Autumn 1968), 1110-1111. Brief personal memoir and tribute.

————. "A Durable Fire: Donald Davidson and the Profession of Letters." *Southern Review,* III (Summer, 1967), 721—41. Eloquent, sympathetic assessment of Davidson's achievement as poet and man of letters.

————. "Meaning and Metaphor in Donald Davidson's 'A Touch of Snow.'" *Southern Review,* II (Summer, 1966), 516—23. Explication of the poem as representative of the poet's best mature work.

CATER, CATHERINE. "Four Voices Out of the South." *Michigan Alumnus Quarterly Review,* L (Winter, 1944), 168–73. Suggests relationships between Southern Agrarianism and Davidson's poetry.

CONNELLY, THOMAS LAWRENCE. "The Vanderbilt Agrarians: Time and Place in Southern Tradition." *Tennessee Historical Quarterly,* XXII (March, 1963), 22–37. The Agrarian movement within a historical context.

COWAN, LOUISE. "Donald Davidson: The 'Long Street.' " William E. Walker and Robert L. Welker, eds. *Reality and Myth: Essays in American Literature in Memory of Richmond Croom Beatty.* Nashville: Vanderbilt University Press, 1964. Analyzes the importance of tradition as a theme in Davidson's poetry; perhaps the best critical essay on the subject.

————. "The Communal World of Southern Literature." *Georgia Review,* XIV (Fall, 1960), 248–57. Nature and themes of modern Southern writing, with a discussion of "Aunt Maria and the Gourds" and "Georgia Pastorals."

————. *The Fugitive Group: A Literary History.* Baton Rouge: Louisiana State University Press, 1959. Authoritative history of *The Fugitive* magazine; recognizes Davidson's position as a cohesive force in the collaboration.

————. "The *Pietas* of Southern Poetry." Louis D. Rubin, Jr., and Robert D. Jacobs, eds. *South: Modern Southern Literature in Its Cultural Setting.* Garden City: Dolphin Books, Doubleday and Company, 1961. Distinguishes poetry of the South from national poetry of the 1920's and 1930's; includes an analysis of "Lines Written for Allen Tate on His Sixtieth Anniversary."

DANIELS, JONATHAN. *A Southerner Discovers the South.* New York: Macmillan Company, 1938. An unsympathetic report of a visit with Davidson in the 1930's.

DAVIS, LOUISE. "He Clings to Enduring Values." Nashville *Tennessean Magazine,* September 4, 1949, pp. 6–8. Informal feature story valuable for its biographical content.

DOYLE, JOHN ROBERT, JR. "Pacing the Long Street with Donald Davidson." *Sewanee Review,* LXXIV (Autumn, 1966), 946–50. Sympathetic assessment.

DRAKE, ROBERT. "Donald Davidson and the Ancient Mariner." *Vanderbilt Alumnus,* XLIX (January–February, 1964), 18–22. Personal impressions of Davidson as a professor and campus personality.

EATON, CHARLES EDWARD. "Donald Davidson and the Dynamics

of Nostalgia." *Georgia Review,* XX (Fall, 1966), 261–69. On the distinctive and unique qualities of Davidson's poetry.

EMERSON, O. B. "Prophet Next Door." William E. Walker and Robert L. Welker, eds. *Reality and Myth: Essays in American Literature in Memory of Richmond Croom Beatty.* Nashville: Vanderbilt University Press, 1964. Mentions Davidson's early influence on the literary reputation of William Faulkner.

FAIN, JOHN TYREE. "Introduction." *The Spyglass: Views and Reviews, 1924–1930.* By Donald Davidson. Nashville: Vanderbilt University Press, 1963. Excellent account of Davidson's years as book editor for the Nashville *Tennessean.*

FLETCHER, JOHN GOULD. "The Modern Southern Poets." *Westminister Magazine,* XXIII (Winter, 1935), 229–51. Early enthusiastic appraisal of the poetry.

GORLIER, CLAUDIO. "Il Sud di un Reazionario: ⟨⟨Donald Davidson⟩⟩." *Questioni,* Anno VIII (January–March, 1960), 52–55. Appreciation by the translator of some of Davidson's poetry into Italian.

HOFFMAN, FREDERICK J., CHARLES ALLEN, CAROLYN ULRICH. *The Little Magazine: A History and a Bibliography.* Princeton: Princeton University Press, 1946. Includes a historical account of *The Fugitive* and Davidson's importance to the endeavor.

INGE, M. THOMAS. "Donald Davidson on Faulkner: An Early Recognition." *Georgia Review,* XX (Winter, 1966), 454–62. Reprints with an introduction Davidson's early perceptive reviews of Faulkner's first three novels.

————. "The Unheeding South: Donald Davidson on James Branch Cabell." *The Cabellian,* II (Autumn, 1969), 17–20. Suggests reasons why Cabell was misunderstood by Davidson and other younger Southern writers.

KARANIKAS, ALEXANDER. *Tillers of a Myth: Southern Agrarians as Social and Literary Critics.* Madison: University of Wisconsin Press, 1966. Poorly researched summary of the major ideas of the Southern Agrarians; only occasional mention of Davidson.

LASSETER, ROLLIN A., III. "The Southern Myth in Donald Davidson's Poetry." *Kentucky Review,* I (Fall, 1967), 31–43. Finds that the poetry is heroic, myth-making poetry drawing upon the sources of Southern history.

MONTGOMERY, MARION. "Bells for John Stewart's Burden." *Georgia Review,* XX (Summer, 1966), 145–81. Caustic criticism of John L. Stewart's *The Burden of Time;* Montgomery includes extensive commentary on Davidson's work.

PRATT, WILLIAM, ed. *The Fugitive Poets: Modern Southern Poets in Perspective.* New York: E. P. Dutton & Co., 1965. The introduction is an admirable concise summary of the significance of the major Fugitives to American literature.

PURDY, ROB ROY, ed. *Fugitives' Reunion: Conversations at Vanderbilt, May 3-5, 1956.* Nashville: Vanderbilt University Press, 1959. Transcripts of informal conversations among the Fugitives on the occasion of their reunion.

RANSOM, JOHN CROWE. "The Most Southern Poet." *Sewanee Review,* LXX (Spring, 1962), 202-7. Recognizes the uncompromising allegiance to regionalism in Davidson's poetry.

ROCK, VIRGINIA, "The Making and Meaning of *I'll Take My Stand:* A Study in Utopian-Conservatism, 1925-1939." Unpublished Ph.D. dissertation, University of Minnesota, 1961. Authoritative cultural and literary history of the Agrarian movement; being revised for publication.

RUBIN, LOUIS D., JR. "Four Southerners." John Russell Brown, Irvin Ehrenpreis, and Bernard Harris, eds. *American Poetry.* New York: St. Martin's Press, 1965. General survey and assessment of the poetry of Ransom, Davidson, Tate, and Warren.

————. "The Concept of Nature in Modern Southern Poetry." *American Quarterly,* IX (Spring, 1957), 63—71. Davidson is among those poets discussed.

————. *The Faraway Country: Writers of the Modern South.* Seattle: University of Washington Press, 1963. Agrarian themes in Davidson's work are mentioned in a chapter on "The Poetry of Agrarianism."

STEWART, JOHN LINCOLN. *The Burden of Time: The Fugitives and Agrarians.* Princeton: Princeton University Press, 1965. Opinionated, often erroneous critical account of the two movements; especially unsympathetic toward Davidson.

STEWART, RANDALL. "Donald Davidson." Louis D. Rubin, Jr., and Robert D. Jacobs, eds. *South: Modern Southern Literature in Its Cultural Setting.* Garden City: Dolphin Books, Doubleday and Company, 1961. Fine critical estimate of the prose and poetry.

TATE, ALLEN. "The Gaze Past, The Glance Present." *Sewanee Review,* LXX (Autumn, 1962), 671—73. Homage to Davidson as "an American poet of perfect independence and integrity," who produced some of the most impressive poetry written since World War I.

WADE, JOHN DONALD. "Oasis." *Sewanee Review,* LXX (Spring, 1962), 208—12. Warm appreciation of Davidson's poetry as "intelligent, learned, original, honest, and noble in point of view."

WARREN, ROBERT PENN. "A Note on Three Southern Poets." *Poetry,* XL (May, 1932), 103—13. Brief criticism of Fletcher, Davidson, and Ransom.

YOUNG, THOMAS DANIEL, and M. THOMAS INGE. "Lee in the
Mountains: The Making of a Poem." *Donald Davidson: An Essay
and a Bibliography.* Nashville: Vanderbilt University Press, 1965.
A textual analysis of the process of revision in the creation of
Davidson's best-known poem.

INDEX